DATE DUE

Praise for *Intelligent Governance for the 21st Century*

"Berggruen and Gardels offer an unconventional take on what good governance should mean in the 21st century, going beyond exasperated accounts of East versus West to offer something far more compelling and pragmatic."

– Eric Schmidt, Executive Chairman, Google

"Berggruen and Gardels seem to be everywhere – from Beijing to Rome to Mexico City – and know everyone, cross-pollinating ideas beyond all kinds of boundaries. And they have the determination and resources to put their highly original and worthy ideas into action."

– Nouriel Roubini, Roubini Associates

"With existing structures of democracy producing widespread alienation, there is an urgent need to reconsider governance in the 21st century. Berggruen and Gardels propose hybrid institutions that combine accountability with expertise, inclusiveness with meritocracy. Bringing together Confucian traditions with a European sense of history and American pragmatism, this is that rare book that combines radically innovative thinking with extensive practical knowledge. It should be on the reading list of anyone – politicians, CEOs – concerned with good governance in a time of globalization."

– John Gray, Emeritus Professor, London School of Economics, author of *The Two Faces of Liberalism*

Intelligent Governance for the 21st Century

Nicolas Berggruen and Nathan Gardels

Intelligent
Governance
for the 21st
Century

A Middle Way between
West and East

polity

First published in 2013 by Polity Press

Polity Press
65 Bridge Street
Cambridge CB2 1UR, UK

Polity Press
350 Main Street
Malden, MA 02148, USA

ISBN-13: 978-0-7456-5973-2

A catalogue record for this book is available from the British Library.

Typeset in 11 on 13 pt Sabon
by Servis Filmsetting Ltd, Stockport, Cheshire
Printed and bound in Great Britain by MPG Books Group Limited, Bodmin,
Cornwall

For further information on Polity, visit our website: www.politybooks.com

Contents

Acknowledgments   vii

Introduction   1

Part I Globalization and Governance

1 Globalization 2.0 and the Challenges to Good
   Governance   7

2 America's Consumer Democracy versus
   China's Modern Mandarinate   21

3 Liberal Democratic Constitutionalism and
   Meritocracy: Hybrid Possibilities   48

4 The New Challenges for Governance: Social
   Networks, Megacities, and the Global
   Scattering of Productive Capabilities   75

**Part II Intelligent Governance: Theory and
Practice**

5 Intelligent Governance: Tenets and Template   103

Contents

6 Rebooting California's Dysfunctional
  Democracy   126

7 The G-20: Global Governance from Summits
  to Subnational Networks   149

8 Europe: Political Union and the Democratic
  Deficit   164

Part III Conclusion

9 Survival of the Wisest   181

Notes   185

Acknowledgments

While the authors are solely responsible for the contents of this book, we have been privileged to draw from the truly remarkable array of leaders and thinkers around the world who have been active members in the three main projects of the Nicolas Berggruen Institute: the Think Long Committee for California, the 21st Century Council, and the Council on the Future of Europe. They are all listed, respectively, in Chapters 6, 7, and 8. Their insights as well as their broad experience in practical governance of their societies have been invaluable in shaping our ideas.

To start with we have to single out Jacques Attali for thanks since he introduced the two of us and is always brimming with stimulating ideas. In California, we are indebted to Bob Hertzberg, former Speaker of the Assembly and "best governor California never had," for his indefatigable energy latched to vision rare in a practical politician. Felipe González, Gerhard Schroeder, Juan Luis Cebrián, and Fernando Henrique Cardoso were instrumental in founding the 21st Century Council. Gordon Brown has brought the same intelligence and global scope to our Council that he brought to his chairmanship of the critical G-20 summit in London when

vii

Acknowledgments

prime minister of the UK during the financial crisis of 2008–9. Mario Monti's labors as prime minister in the "depoliticized space" of a technocratic government in Italy have been in many ways a test of our approach to governance, and we have deeply appreciated the opportunity to exchange ideas with him in the European context.

We particularly value what we've learned from our Chinese colleagues – Zheng Bijian, Wu Jianmin, Zhang Yi, and Feng Wei in Beijing – and have taken Zheng's strategic theme of "building on a convergence of interests to create a community of interests" as a guiding light of our global endeavors.

The powerful cross-pollination of ideas between the Eastern and Western scholars whom Li Chenyang and Daniel A. Bell gathered together at Singapore's Nanyang Technical University in January 2012 to discuss political meritocracy was almost mind-bending. There is far too little of that kind of in-depth engagement of worldviews today. We benefited from it greatly.

Our association with Google's Eric Schmidt and Jared Cohen has opened wide a window into the impact of the information revolution and social media on governance. Our proximity here in California to Silicon Valley has enabled us to hold several discussions to delve more deeply into these subjects. We are highly grateful to all the participants in those meetings in the Bay Area, which included Microsoft strategist Charles Songhurst, MIT Media Lab director Joichi Ito, e-Bay founders Jeff Skoll and Pierre Omidyar, YouTube creator Chad Hurley, Twitter founder Jack Dorsey, and Google.org's Shona Brown and Matthew Stepka. At various times those discussions were also joined by California Governor Jerry Brown; Francis Fukuyama; the US State Department's top digital diplomat, Alec Ross; *Transparent Society*

Acknowledgments

author David Brin; and Singapore's former foreign minister, George Yeo.

Finally, we are profoundly thankful to Dawn Nakagawa, Executive Director of the Nicolas Berggruen Institute, without whose logistical genius, professionalism, steady nerves during inevitable crises, and persistence we would be lost.

Introduction

In this book we examine how the best practices of governance in East and West, developed over centuries under very different historical and cultural circumstances, might be brought to bear on the common challenges wrought by globalization.

We focus on China and the United States, not as literal alternatives, but as a metaphor of the trade-offs that must be considered in constructing a mixed constitutional system that incorporates the signature elements of both – respectively, guidance by the long-term perspective of meritocratic elites and the popular sovereignty of democracy.

In the first chapter, "Globalization 2.0 and the Challenges to Good Governance," we contrast the geopolitical and geo-civilizational outlooks of West and East as they face the transition underway from American-led globalization to an interdependence of plural identities. We also introduce the concept of "intelligent governance" in response to the political and cultural awakening that is part and parcel of the global shift. Our argument is that good governance must *devolve* power and *involve* citizens more meaningfully in ruling their communities while legitimizing

1

the delegation of authority through *decision-division* to institutions that can capably manage the systemic links of integration.

In Chapter 2, "America's Consumer Democracy versus China's Modern Mandarinate," we analyze the contemporary strengths and deficiencies of both systems.

Chapter 3, "Liberal Democratic Constitutionalism and Meritocracy: Hybrid Possibilities," revisits the debates over the qualities of political meritocracy versus electoral democracy as forms of good governance, touching on topics from the origins of the examination system in China to the deliberations of the American Founding Fathers over the pitfalls of direct democracy.

We further muse over some of the affinities of Western classical and Enlightenment thinkers with Confucian precepts and ponder what the building blocks of a hybrid form of governance might be where rulers are selected on merit but checked by popular elections.

Having revisited the old debates, in Chapter 4 we place them in the context of the newest challenges and opportunities of the 21st century – social networks, the emergence of the megacity, and the global scattering of productive capabilities – to which all systems of governance must respond.

Taking all of the foregoing into consideration, Chapter 5, "Intelligent Governance: Tenets and Template," is an exercise in political imagination that proposes an institutional design for a middle way between West and East – not a one-size-fits-all blueprint, but an ideal suggestion, the principles of which would have to be molded to particular circumstance.

In Chapters 6, 7, and 8 we report on our efforts to do just that – adapt the principles of intelligent governance in widely varying conditions, from California to the G-20 to Europe.

Introduction

Chapter 9 puts our discussion in the broadest possible historical context of the potential emergence of the first truly global civilization – if we figure out how to make our different operating systems compatible. Our title, "Survival of the Wisest," says it all.

Since the book is about live, ongoing projects, the reader may follow the activities of the Nicolas Berggruen Institute at http://www.berggrueninstitute.org.

Nicholas Berggruen
Nathan Gardels
Los Angeles/Paris, June 2012

Part I

Globalization and Governance

1

Globalization 2.0 and the Challenges to Good Governance

Introduction

"East is East, West is West." But, today, the twain are intertwined.

Everyone knows the contrasting traits that distinguish these broad civilizational spheres: authority versus freedom, the community versus the individual, the cycles of the ages versus the progress of history, and representative democracy versus, in China's case, rule by a meritocratic mandarinate. Yet, we also know that China has become the factory of the world and the largest creditor of the United States.

In this book we revisit the twain that Rudyard Kipling famously said "never shall meet" in this new historical context where China and the West are as tightly tethered as they remain highly distinct.

As the West recedes from its centuries-long dominance and the Middle Kingdom regains its solid foothold in history, we are obliged to look out on this changing landscape with Eastern as well as Western lenses.

If the reader will permit the reduction of some essential truths, the modern Western mind tends to see contradiction between irreconcilable opposites that can only be resolved by the dominance of one over the other. Following the German idealist philosopher Georg Wilhelm Friedrich Hegel,[1] this was the approach Francis Fukuyama[2] took when he argued that "the end of history" had arrived after the Cold War in the triumph of liberal democracy over other forms of human governance. In the geopolitical mind of the West, territories and ideologies are either won or lost.

The Eastern mind instead sees complementary aspects of a whole – yin and yang in Taoist parlance – that must be continually balanced on a pragmatic basis depending on shifting conditions. History doesn't end. The cycles go on as the relationships between freedom and authority or the individual and the community find a new equilibrium. In the "geo-civilizational" mind of the East, what is incommensurate can co-exist.

When he quips that "the Tao is much deeper than Hegel," George Yeo, the former foreign minister of Singapore and one of Asia's most important thinker/practitioners, is alluding to this contrast between the Eastern and Western mind.

It is from within the perspective expressed by Yeo that this book addresses the common challenges of governance that both East and West are facing as a result of the complexity and diversity of the interdependence that ties us together.

Following the pragmatic, non-ideological Eastern approach, our concern is what we can learn from each other. The question is not whether rule by a meritocratic mandarinate rooted in China's ancient "institutional civilization" will win out over Western-style democracy, or vice versa. The question we pose is what balanced combination of meritocracy and democracy, of authority and freedom, of community and the individual, can create the healthiest body politic and the most intelligent form of governance for the 21st century. Indeed, we ponder whether there might even be the emergent possibility of a new "middle way."

Is Democracy Self-Correcting?

The conventional, though not incorrect, wisdom in the West is that, despite the awesome achievement of lifting hundreds of millions of people out of poverty in just three decades, the modern mandarinate of nominally Communist China is not self-correcting, and thus not sustainable. Unless it loosens its autocratic grip by allowing freer expression and more democratic mechanisms for popular feedback and accountability, the "red dynasty" will succumb to terminal political decay – rife corruption, arbitrary abuse by authorities, and stagnation – just as all previous dynasties have in China's millennial history.

The unconventional observation of this book is that, just as we've seen with financial markets, Western democracy is no more self-correcting than China's system. In a mirror image of China's challenge, one-person-one-vote electoral democracy embedded in a consumer culture of immediate gratification is also headed for terminal political decay unless it reforms. Taking a cue from China's experience with meritocratic rule, establishing capable institutions that embody both the perspective of the long term and common good in governance is key to the sustainability of the democratic West. The argument we will make in this book is that restoring equilibrium in each system will require a recalibration of political settings through mixed constitutions that combine *knowledgeable democracy* with *accountable meritocracy*.

9

Governance

Governance is about how the cultural habits, political institutions, and economic system of a society can be aligned to deliver the desired good life for its people. Good governance is when these structures combine in a balance that produces effective and sustainable results in the common interest. Bad governance results either when underlying conditions have so changed that once effective practices become dysfunctional or when political decay sets in as organized special interests gain dominance – or both. Then debts and deficits become unsustainable, protective cartels sap the vigor of the economy, corruption destroys trust, social mobility stagnates, and inequality grows. The ruling consensus loses legitimacy. Decline sets in.

Dysfunction and decay aptly describe governance across much of the democratic West today, which is in crisis from its ancient birthplace in Greece to its most advanced outpost in California. After centuries of forward momentum fueled by an inner civilizational confidence, debt, political gridlock, indecisiveness, and fraying legitimacy are paralyzing the capacity of liberal democracy and free market economies to manage change. On the face of it, that momentum and confidence has shifted to the East. Indeed, as we have already noted, Western liberal democracy is being challenged as the best form of governance by non-Western forms of modernity, most notably by China's mandarinate and state-led capitalism. Yet signs of decay and dysfunction are already appearing there as well owing to enveloping corruption and the collateral social, environmental, and even spiritual damage of China's remarkable success.

10

Globalization 2.0

From Globalization 1.0 to 2.0

The challenges produced by the present global power shift, combined with rapid technological advance, are daunting for the rising powers no less than for the receding ones. All political systems are in some way experiencing disequilibrium as they seek to adjust to the repeated shocks caused by the transition underway from what we call Globalization 1.0 to Globalization 2.0.

In the decades since the end of the Cold War, American-led globalization – 1.0 – has so thoroughly transformed the world through the freer flow of trade, capital, information, and technology that it has given birth to a new phase – Globalization 2.0.

"In the past few centuries what was once the European and then the American periphery became the core of the world economy," writes *Financial Times* analyst Martin Wolf. "Now, the economies of the periphery are re-emerging as the core. This is transforming the entire world . . . this is far and away the biggest single fact about our world."[3]

Nobel economist Michael Spence reinforces this point. What we are seeing today, he writes, are "two parallel and interacting revolutions: the continuation of the industrial Revolution in the advanced countries, and the sudden and dramatic spreading pattern of growth in the developing world. One could call the second revolution the Inclusiveness Revolution. After two centuries of high-speed divergence, a pattern of convergence has taken over."[4]

This great economic and technological *convergence* that is the consequence of Globalization 1.0 has at the same time given birth to a new cultural *divergence* as the wealthier emerging powers look to their civilizational foundations to define themselves anew against

11

the waning hegemony of the West. Since economic strength engenders cultural and political self-assertion, Globalization 2.0, above all, means the interdependence of plural identities instead of one model for all. The once regnant Western liberal democracies must now contend on the world stage not only with neo-Confucian China but also with the likes of the Islamic-oriented democracy within Turkey's secular framework, which has become an attractive template for the newly liberated Arab street. In short, the world is returning to the "normal pluralism" that has characterized most of human history.

Historically, a power shift of this magnitude often ends in collision and conflict. But, given the intensive integration that the post-Cold War round of globalization has wrought, it also poses entirely new possibilities of cooperation and cross-pollination across a plural civilizational landscape.

We are thus at an historical crossroads. How we govern ourselves in the coming decades within and among nations will determine which of these paths the 21st century follows.

Establishing a new equilibrium under the Globalization 2.0 operating system is a double challenge.

The complexity of the deeper global integration of trade, investment, production, and consumption, no less information flows, requires greater political and technical capacity at the megacity-region, national, and supranational level to manage the systemic links of interdependence. If it all falls apart, everyone will be damaged. At the same time, the growing diversity that has come with the global spread of wealth, amplified by the participatory power of social media, requires more devolution of power toward the grass roots, where the restive public is clamoring from the bottom up for a say in the rules that govern their lives. Political awakenings everywhere are demanding the dignity of meaningful participation.

Failure to find an institutional response to this double challenge will result in a crisis of legitimacy for any governing system – either because of the failure to perform through providing inclusive growth and employment or because a "democratic deficit" that shuts out diverse public voices will undermine effective consent.

Getting the balance right will thus make the difference between dynamic and stalled societies as well as determine whether clash or cooperation emerges as the global *modus operandi*.

That balance might be called "intelligent governance," which devolves power and meaningfully involves citizens in matters of their competence while fostering legitimacy and consent for delegated authority at higher levels of complexity. Devolving, involving, and decision-division are the key elements of intelligent governance that will reconcile knowledgeable democracy with accountable meritocracy.

What the right balance is will differ because political systems are at different starting points. Every system must reboot based on the cultural settings of its present operating system. While China, as the conventional wisdom suggests, would need more participatory involvement and a more accountable meritocratic mandarinate to achieve balance, the United States would need a more depoliticized democracy in which governance for the long term and common good is insulated from the populist short-term, special interest political culture of one-person-one-vote elections. In short, China would need to lighten up while the US would need to tighten up.

In Europe, the institutional infrastructure necessary

to complete integration – a strong but limited political union – must be invested with democratic legitimacy or it will fail to attract the allegiance of European citizens who are disenfranchised and thus disenchanted.

As the adjustment mechanism of the global power shift underway, the G-20, like the institutions of the European Union, must similarly be invested with legitimacy by nation-states and their publics. Otherwise it will lack the political capacity to provide the global public goods – a reserve currency, the stability of trade and financial flows, security, nuclear non-proliferation, and measures to combat climate change – that no individual hegemonic state or set of international states can provide under the multi-polar order of Globalization 2.0. Since proximity confers legitimacy, the chief challenge here is how to spin networks of "subnational" localities into a web of global governance as the 21st-century alternative to the outmoded notion of a distant and oppressive "world Leviathan."

This book seeks to address this central issue of the first half of the 21st century: how good governance can establish equilibrium within nations as well as among them at the regional and global level.

To do so, we will examine the contending systems of what we call America's "consumer democracy" and China's "modern mandarinate" as a metaphor for identifying the tradeoffs that are required to achieve the proper balance of good governance. We will further propose an "ideal, mixed constitutional template" that is a hybrid of meritocracy and democracy. No armchair theorists, we will then report on our practical experience in implementing such a template in widely varying circumstances from California to Europe to the G-20 level.

The ultimate point of this book is that governance

14

matters in whether societies move forward or backward. Never has that been more true than during this transition from Globalization 1.0 to 2.0. If cities, states, or nations can't navigate the rushing white waters of change, they will crash against the rocky shoals or be left behind in stagnant waters.

A BRIEF INVENTORY OF DISEQUILIBRIUM

Everyone is feeling the shock waves of change. In the United States, Joseph Schumpeter's[5] famous "destruction" seems to be racing so far ahead of "creation" that the growing inequality between those moving ahead and those left behind is undermining faith both in democracy and in capitalism, pitting the "99 percent against the 1 percent" at the top of the income scale. Partisan gridlock has become the norm, dividing democracy against itself and paralyzing the ability of political leaders to act.

Across the spectrum in Europe, Japan, and the US, debts and deficits anchor the political imagination to the past. Everyone's dreams are being deleveraged.

Disunity in the Eurozone over resolving the sovereign debt crisis has called the historic project of integration as well as the European social contract itself into question. To regain its balance, Europe has to go all the way back to the nation-state or all the way forward to political union. Ignoring demise instead of facing it, Japan is coasting into a retirement trap on the basis of its accumulated wealth. The country is drawing down on its domestic savings, with little thought of how to re-energize itself for the next generation.

In China, the imperatives of the middle-class transition that must shift away from the investment/

---

export model of growth toward domestic consumption, all the while coping with the collateral social and environmental damage of quick-paced development, are testing the mettle of its so far highly successful market-Leninist mandarinate. Most spectacularly, Arab autocrats have fallen like dominoes before the networked rage of "Facebook youth" and the resurgence of repressed Islamists. Even in Singapore, arguably the best-governed place on the planet, the long-ruling Lee Kuan Yew style of paternalist democracy has not been spared the rising discontent of that nanny state's ever-less passive citizens.

At the global level, the G-20's capacity for global governance is perennially hampered in its efforts to correct global imbalances by sovereign hesitations. Local and global remain in a stand-off even as enlightened self-interest in reigniting global growth would reasonably dictate more robust cooperation.

In short, every system is struggling to re-establish equilibrium in the emergent post-American order. Grasping how the present imbalances arose as a consequence of greater global integration and technological advance is key to figuring out what kind of governing institutions are best suited to move beyond the current crisis.

An exhaustive analysis of how we got from there to here is beyond the scope of this book. But a simple sketch will help set the stage for our discussion of governance.

American-led "neo-liberal" Globalization 1.0 spread the wealth globally, if unequally, in the wake of the end of the Cold War. Markets were opened. Billions of new workers were invited in and started climbing the income ladder out of poverty. The spread of new information technologies dramatically enhanced productivity. For much of the West, less so for Germany and Japan, which retained their manufacturing and engineering base, this double development had the effect of hollowing out the middle class even as the global scale of markets and liberalized regulation enabled an unprecedented concentration of wealth for some, notably in the American financial sector, which, by 2005, accounted for 40 percent all business profits.[6]

Symptomatic of the effects across the board on the manufacturing sector, cheap Chinese labor, supply-chain savvy, microchip technology, and robotics conjoined to displace the very jobs upon which the American middle class was built.

According to an influential study by a group of economists in 2012, one quarter of the "aggregate decline of US manufacturing employment" over the past two decades was due to trade with China.[7]

In 1960, General Motors employed 595,000 workers. Yet, for all their globe-straddling vibrancy and billions in revenues, the Googles and Twitters of today produce few jobs. Facebook, for example, which has 1 billion daily unique hits, has only 3,500 employees. Apple employs only 43,000 people in the US, mostly in design, while the actual manufacturing of its iPhone takes place in China by Foxconn, which employs 1.2 million workers.[8]

As Michael Spence[9] has shown, 90 percent of the 27 million new jobs created over the last 20 years in the United States instead were generated in the non-tradable sector, mainly lower wage jobs in retail, health care, and government service, many of the latter now slashed by deleveraging budget cuts due to the belated impact of the recession on state and local government revenues. By all accounts, higher

17

education was the greatest factor in the income gap that grew between those who held these sub-prime jobs and those in information technology, design, and other high-value added sectors.

By 2009, according to former IMF chief economist Raghuram Rajan,[10] 58 percent of income in the US was held by the top 1 percent of the population. Since 1975, he reports, the wages of the top 10 percent have grown 65 percent more than the bottom 10 percent. Though exacerbated by tax cuts for the rich during the administration of George W. Bush, the structural cause of the widening income chasm has been mainly due to the creation–destruction dynamism of a wage-deflating globalized labor market and the labor-displacing productivity of new technology.

Rajan further argues that this demotion of the American middle class was concealed by the housing bubble driven by globally available liquidity, largely from China's savings, which suppressed long-term interest rates, abetted by the lax credit policies of the US Federal Reserve that held up home prices until the bubble burst in 2009. In effect, keeping up with the Joneses was based not on increased income from decent paying jobs, but from borrowing that falling income could not sustain when home prices fell.

Just as the housing bubble in the US sustained the myth of upward mobility, low interest rates linked through the euro to German prudence and productivity along with flush global liquidity broadly enabled European states, mainly in the southern tier, to sustain a level of social welfare and public services beyond their means to afford it. The sovereign debt implosion has now exposed that gap.

For China, Globalization 1.0 meant hundreds of millions made their way out of marginal subsistence,

18

were drawn to megacities where, for the first time in history, 50 percent of Chinese now live, and set on a path toward middle class status. That in turn has put immense pressure on the authoritarian development model to accommodate both the aspirations of that rising middle class for more openness and accountability and the left-behind migrant and rural poor for greater equality. The demand for the rule of law against arbitrary and unfairly compensated land seizures from peasant villagers has erupted into open rebellion across China, most famously in the case of Wukan in 2011. Revolts over industrial pollution, such as that in Haimen in Guandong province around the same time, are also common across China today.

Even for the most prosperous, the fevered materialism of gloriously getting rich has led many to question the spiritual price of such a single-minded pursuit of prosperity, in turn giving rise to a Confucian renaissance seeking a renewed ethical foundation for Chinese society.

Overall, just as the division of labor in manufacturing a product like Apple's iPad has been spread across designers, suppliers, and assemblers globally – confounding the very measurement of "trade balances" – the old notions of First and Third Worlds have been fused by Globalization 1.0 into hybrid realities of rich countries with poor people and poor countries with rich people. The integration of large city-regions as production hubs in the global division of labor is emptying out the hinterlands and creating massive population centers – megacities the size of entire nations, particularly in the emerging economies.

Seeking to adjust to these dislocations, China is plotting a path toward middle-class transition while the US is realizing the need for a middle-class restoration. As we will discuss more thoroughly in the next chapter, the discontent of both the rising and falling middle classes across the globe has been able to find broad and easy expression with the advent of social networking media, mobilizing dissatisfaction in every guise, from the Tea Party to Occupy Wall Street to the "Facebook children" of Tahrir Square, the *indignados* in Spain, and the raucous *weibo* microbloggers in China.

The question of how we get from here to the future poses a series of paradoxes because the practices and institutions that have worked so far are now the very impediments to moving forward.

Only by recalibrating the settings of political systems in order to establish good governance can we escape this cross-cutting paralysis.

2

America's Consumer Democracy versus China's Modern Mandarinate

Introduction

Zhang Weiwei, a former interpreter for Deng Xiaoping and author of *The China Wave: The Rise of a Civilizational State*,[1] is surely right that, because of China's stunningly successful rise, the key debate of the coming decades will no longer focus on democracy versus autocracy or meritocracy, as it did from the 18th to the 20th century. Instead, he argues, it will be over what constitutes good governance versus bad governance.

Our aim in this book is not to cheerlead for the Chinese or the American system. It is to assess which features of each can best contribute to good governance or will lead to bad governance as we navigate the transition from Globalization 1.0 to 2.0.

An exhaustive comparison of political systems, from India's creaking bureaucratic democracy to Europe's faltering social market arrangement, is beyond the scope of this book. What we will do is examine the relative weaknesses and strengths of what we call America's consumer democracy and China's modern mandarinate as a way to parse the key elements that are required to

21

achieve the kind of tradeoffs in governance that will be required in the evolving geo-civilizational landscape of the 21st century.

We will look at each in turn and then ask whether, despite the vastly different cultural settings, both East and West can benefit from adapting in their own way the successful features of the other.

At the outset of the 20th century, Sun Yat-Sen, the father of modern China, sought to blend the institutions of Western democracy with Confucian meritocracy. Perhaps today, as the "rise of the rest" challenges Western dominance, the political imagination may again be open to new ideas. This time, it won't just be Western ideas flowing East, but Eastern ideas flowing West as well – as was the case to such an extent when the West was rising in the 18th century that some European scholars regarded Confucius as the "patron saint of the Enlightenment" because he extolled government by the meritorious and enlightened against both mob and monarch.

Although both China and America have "capitalist" economies, their governing operating systems could not be more different. America's operating system today is what we call a "consumer democracy." China's operating system is a quasi-meritocratic mandarinate. And, of course, America is a mature economy and China, though the second biggest economy in the world, is still largely poor and developing.

In essence, America's "consumer democracy" has a one-person-one-vote political system aimed at creating the greatest space for personal freedom and free markets in order to best enable the pursuit of happiness – more or less defined in our time as meeting the demand for short-term immediate gratification of the consumer culture. The central government is checked by the rule of law and balanced by a division of powers among the executive, legislative, and judicial branches as well as by the autonomy of states. Until the 2008–9 financial crisis, the regnant wisdom was that markets were self-regulating and self-correcting. Government is thus seen as a necessary evil, not a necessary good.

Though solely ruled by a nominal Communist Party, China's governing operating system is rooted in what the Peking University scholar Pan Wei calls the Middle Kingdom's "institutional civilization."[2] Often referred to as "neo-Confucian," it draws on the millennial heritage of pragmatic rule by learned and experienced elites – mandarins – based on merit, not by the choice of the public. In the post-Mao era, no one in the collective leadership makes it to the top without first being tested by tough assignments in the provinces, trained in the Central Party School and vetted by the Party's Organization Department. Government is seen as a necessary virtue, not at all an evil. Its chief aim is to promote stability and prosperity in the name of the common good, even as it unleashes the fervent materialism of "getting rich gloriously." Insulated from the short-term pressures of popular elections and with command over vast resources, the modern mandarinate charts out a decades-long path ahead for the country.

Personal liberty and freedom of expression are subordinated to those goals. Following China's Confucian heritage, officials (ideally) are morally obliged to serve the general welfare of citizens instead – so far – of being held accountable to them by the rule of law. Rule *by* law instead of rule *of* law is the norm. Though the economy is subject to market forces, both internally and globally, the strong hand of the state guides the market through interventionist industrial policies, currency manipulation, and extensive regulation. Fully 60 percent of the largest industries are state-controlled. As Party ideologist Hu Qili said as long ago as 1987, "the West has no patent right on the market."[3]

Whereas the question for America is whether the political system of one-person-one-vote democracy embedded in a consumer culture is capable of self-correction and renewal, the question for China is whether the modern mandarinate of the Communist Party is capable of maintaining forward momentum in the 21st century without more democratic feedback mechanisms beyond the repressive tolerance of its "monitory webocracy" – the massive popular pressure of netizens that we will discuss in Chapter 4. Is authoritarian modernization from above, which has been so demonstrably effective in guiding China's investment and export-led growth for the last three decades, capable of making the transition to a complex, wired, consumerist middle-class society, or must it yield to modernization from below?

Critiques and Comparisons

"Democracy is the worst form of government, except for all those other forms that have been tried from time to time," Churchill famously said in the House of Commons in 1947. The prestige of the great British statesman who held forth when the empire was already on its last legs was such that his view has remained the conventional wisdom ever since.

In a way, Churchill pre-figured Francis Fukuyama, who declared the "end of history"[4] in 1989, postulating that the defeat of communism in the Cold War meant the triumph of Western-style liberal democracy suitable for all of humanity.

24

Perhaps now it is time to take another look at democracy as we know it, not just because of the sustained success of forms of non-Western modernity, notably in places like Singapore or China, but because the West itself has changed.

Fukuyama himself has adjusted his historical verdict. In a special issue of the *Financial Times* on China in 2010, he wrote:

> There is a deeper problem with the American model that is nowhere close to being solved. China adapts quickly, making difficult decisions and implementing them effectively. Americans pride themselves on constitutional checks and balances, based on a political culture that distrusts centralised government. This system has ensured individual liberty and a vibrant private sector, but it has now become polarised and ideologically rigid. At present it shows little appetite for dealing with the long-term fiscal challenges the US faces. Democracy in America may have an inherent legitimacy that the Chinese system lacks, but it will not be much of a model to anyone if the government is divided against itself and cannot govern. During the 1989 Tiananmen protests, student demonstrators erected a model of the Statue of Liberty to symbolise their aspirations. Whether anyone in China would do the same at some future date will depend on how Americans address their problems in the present.[5]

In a conversation with Martin Wolf, Fukuyama further scored the suspicion of meritocratic government in Western liberal societies.

> That's actually a big problem in western public administration because good governance is a kind of aristocratic phenomenon. And, we don't like deference to experts and we don't like delegating authority to experts. Therefore, we ring them around with all of these rules,

which limit their discretion, because we don't trust them. This disease has gone furthest in the United States.[6]

In a discussion with California Governor Jerry Brown and others organized by the Nicolas Berggruen Institute in 2011, Fukuyama further lamented how liberal democracy in the US has decayed into a dysfunctional "vetocracy."[7] Following Mancur Olson's central thesis in his seminal *The Rise and Decline of Nations*,[8] Fukuyama argued that well-organized special interest groups bent on preserving their share of the spoils have, through lobbying and campaign contributions, captured the budget and lawmaking process. Whether public employee unions or financial firms fending off regulation, their say, or veto, far outweighs that of unorganized individual voters.

"Vetocracy," says, Fukuyama, "actually prevents governance and produces deficits." This point resonated deeply with Governor Brown, who was unable in 2011 to persuade the required two-thirds of the California legislature even to allow the public to vote on a tax increase.

Instead of being able to invest in the common future as China has been doing, the political system in California, as in the US as a whole, ends up pandering to short-term populist sentiments and serving those with the clout to make sure their interests prevail. In this sense, democracy is a vote for the past because it is a vote for the vested interests of the present.

Fukuyama's critique fairly accords with the view of Chinese critics who argue against introducing one-person-one-vote liberal democracy in that vast nation precisely because its inevitable capture by "the short-term and special interests" would undermine the ability of the state to decisively advance the general interest over the long term. For these critics, China would never have been able to achieve the miracle of its unprecedented rapid economic development through democracy. For them, liberal democracy is hardly the future; it is on its way to being a short-lived experiment in the long history of civilizations.

The Shanghai scholar/entrepreneur Eric X. Li is one who sees "democracy's coming demise." "The American democracy is 92 years old [i.e. since women's suffrage in 1920] – so far still shorter than China's shortest dynasty," Li has written.[9] "Why, then, do so many boldly claim they have discovered the ideal political system for all mankind and that its success is forever assured?" He continued:

> The Americans today are not dissimilar to the Soviets of the last century in that both have seen their political systems and their underlying ideologies as ultimate ends. The Chinese are on the opposite path of pragmatism and will be more or less democratic depending on the results. History does not bode well for the American path.

Of course, there are plenty who reasonably doubt whether the best and brightest at the top in China can continue that nation's amazing path forward as it modernizes as a society and matures into a more complex, advanced economy. It is well known that corruption is beyond rife, particularly at the local level, and especially in the wake of China's nearly trillion dollar stimulus after the global financial crisis of 2008–9. Public resentment has grown against the privileges of the princeling progeny of Party chiefs as well as the arrogant *nouveaux riches*, who are quaffing more fine Bordeaux than anyone else on the planet. Because of the crony connections with developers and lack of accountability, revolts have spread across China against the arbitrary authority and corruption of local officials. Over 230 million microblog *weibo* users register their dissatisfaction daily over issues from the Wenzhou bullet train crash* to tainted milk or pollution in Beijing, even as official polls show that nearly 70 percent of the public think China is going in the right direction.

Critics note that while guiding massive state investment in infrastructure can lead to rapid growth in the beginning, that can turn into a vast waste of resources in overbuilding while urgent needs go unmet for a viable safety net and healthcare. Everyone knows about the entire "empty cities" like Ordos in Inner Mongolia and the 80 million unoccupied housing units that are deflating the real estate bubble and posing the threat of a "hard landing" after years of spectacular growth.[10] None of this is to speak of the continuing crackdown on dissidents, whether innocuous or famous, such as the artist Ai Weiwei, which has led former president Bill Clinton to famously declare that "China is on the wrong side of history."[11]

China may well be on the "wrong side of history" with respect to individual liberty, but America's place on history's right side, and liberal democracy's role, is not at all guaranteed. Historical conditions have changed, both within the United States and in the world around it. Despite the vaunted capacity of democracies to self-correct, that may be no less of a myth than the free market's ability to do so.

The United States today is no longer what common coinage refers to as an "industrial democracy," just as it is not the agriculture-based landed aristocracy in which

---

* After the Wenzhou crash of July 2011, the Chinese blogosphere ignited with comments about the lack of safety of China's vaunted bullet trains and rumors of a coverup of the causes.

the American political system and its constitution were originally conceived – and from which it has scarcely evolved, despite Thomas Jefferson's well-known view that constitutions normally run their course within about 20 years. He felt the living, not the dead, should make the rules by which they are governed.

Far from the insulated homogeneity and small scale of traditional societies with their earthy virtues of place, or even from the time when capital and labor confronted each other across the barricades or through disciplined mass parties, today America is a highly diverse, culturally hybrid, urbanized, and densely networked "consumer democracy" that is predominantly middle class. The United States has become a largely service and information economy where consumer purchases account for 70 percent of gross domestic product.

Above all, the practice of one-person-one-vote electoral democracy has not come to grips with the long-term consequences of its post-World War II marriage to the ideology of consumerism.

Democratic systems are designed to give the majority what they want when they want it. Americans want their liberty and their right to the pursuit of happiness, often reductively defined as consumer plenitude. And they want it now.

By nature, consumer choice is short term and self-interested. Particularly after winning the Cold War against a Soviet regime that sacrificed the present well-being of its people for the "pink clouds of utopia," in poet Yevgeny Yevtushenko's[12] phrase, the triumphant culture of the American superpower willfully forgot how to remember the future. It was confident that electoral democracy and free choice in the marketplace would guide society to the right place in history.

Amplified by the new technologies of the information

age, this dynamic of self-interested choice has largely driven the "Facebook & friends" power shift which is devolving social, cultural, and political authority downward and outward toward diverse networks of the like-minded, organized minorities and the individual.

While no one would diminish the very considerable comforts and conveniences of consumerism, a guiding societal ethos of short-term self-interest inevitably tends to eclipse any perspective of the long-term and common good. All the feedback signals in a consumer democracy – politics, the media and the market – steer behavior toward immediate gratification.

In this Diet Coke culture, all too many, as revealed, for example, by the sub-prime mortgage bubble, have come to expect consumption without savings or education, infrastructure and social security without taxes, just as they expect sweetness without calories in a soft drink. It is easy to see from this dynamic how the "retail rationality" of self-interest can add up to the "wholesale madness" of exuberant bubbles, mountains of debt, and fiscal crisis.

Pandering to this cultural ethos of immediate gratification, politics has become about the next election instead of the next generation. Partisan acrimony rooted in ideological rigidity vies for allegiance of the extremes who determine the outcome of elections in which the apathetic abstain and the centrist disdain. Short-term populist sentiment manipulated by special-interest money sanctioned by the US Supreme Court as "free speech" has further corrupted representative as well as direct democracy. Election campaigns are too easily manipulated by those with the resources to distort honest discourse.

This grip of short-term special interests is so tight that, even after scoring a huge popular mandate in the wake of the 2008–9 financial crash, President Barack Obama was unable, some say unwilling, to re-regulate the "too big to fail" banking system that ignited the crisis. The largest firms, such as Bank of America and JP Morgan, now have even more assets than before. Former Reagan budget director David Stockman[13] has blamed America's version of "crony capitalism" for this since the same personnel pass through the revolving door between the White House and Wall Street, leveraging the political system to protect a worldview that coincides with their private interests.

Democracy as it has evolved in the United States thus appears no more self-correcting than free markets, which, as George Soros[14] has exhaustively argued, tend toward disequilibrium, not equilibrium.

Further, the 24/7 cycle of the media stirs up populist sentiment and serves up prurient fare in order to "monetize" the attention of consumers poised to flip the channel or click the mouse. Social media ties more tightly together than ever before tribes of the likeminded. Deliberation over the big issues diminishes as media platforms evolve to the small mobile screen designed for convenient chats with friends or streaming entertainment videos. Though continuously connected, communication is less and less outside one's niche. Textistentialism has become the practical philosophy: I text, therefore I am. As social scientists have long predicted, greater bandwidth has narrowed the scope of information.

Too many companies that once built their wealth steadily through reinvestment over a quarter of a century focus ever more on the quarterly report and even the daily stock price. The financial sector thrives as much by seeking instantaneous profits through exploiting the small spread in large trades as by matching capital to investment needs.

31

Nearly 40 years ago, long before the credit bubble that nearly took down the financial system when it burst, the late sociologist Daniel Bell presciently theorized in his seminal work *The Cultural Contradictions of Capitalism*[15] that easy credit and the immediacy of consumerism would undermine the discipline of deferred gratification and hard work that has made liberal capitalism the greatest engine of prosperity in history. The economist Dambisa Moyo[16] has similarly noted that by sinking more resources into single family homes and cars than into public infrastructure and other investments, the future America has undermined its ability to compete with those emerging economies, particularly China, that have done so.

In a consumer democracy, as Bell foresaw, there is scarce political capacity for disciplined deferral of gratification and the long-term thinking, planning, and continuity of governance that go with it.

As Michael Hiltzik[17] asks in his book *Colossus*, could America today muster the vision, will, and resources to invest in massive infrastructure projects like the Hoover Dam?

As is often the case, the extreme reveals the essence. Everyone can see that the experience of unmediated direct democracy in California, where popular initiatives dominate governance, has proven ruinous. This valued venue of public recourse, originally designed to counter the power of the state's railroad barons in the early 20th century, has become instead the preserve of special interests and short-term populism. As former California Supreme Court Justice Ron George asks rhetorically: "Has the voter initiative now become the tool of the very special interests it was intended to control, and an impediment to the effective functioning of a true democratic society?"[18]

The combination of special interest pleading and the short-term voter mentality has tied state finances in knots by locking in costs and locking out revenues. Unable to bridge the partisan divide and the grip of special interests, the legislature has compounded the problem through short-term stop-gap measures and extensive borrowing. As a result, California today is mired in debt and political gridlock. A series of initiatives over the years that have cut property taxes and sought to punish criminals shows how rational self-interest at the ballot box can add up to the wholesale irrationality of unintended consequences: the California that used to be thought of as the "Golden State" of opportunity now spends more on prisons than on higher education (11 percent and 7.5 percent of the 2011 budget, respectively), undermining the very foundations of the future.[19]

Absent significant reform in the way governance is conducted, California faces annual budget shortfalls in the billions. Populist over-reliance on the narrow tax base of upper-end income means budgets are flush in good years, but must be slashed when there is an economic downturn. No revenue cushion puts away resources for the bad times. All revenue is spent as it comes in. Traders consider California's bonds to be a greater risk than those of Kazakhstan. Already nearly 8 percent of the state's budget goes to debt service. As in London and Athens, students are protesting tuition increases and canceled classes. Elementary school teachers are being laid off. Prisoners are being let go. (In May 2011, the US Supreme Court ordered the release of more than 30,000 felons because their human rights were being violated through overcrowding.) Health services for the poor and elderly are being slashed.[20]

Worse, California has not invested substantially in

infrastructure for the last five decades, since the late 1950s and early 1960s, when it built Pharoanic-scale canals to bring water from the wet north to the arid south, a world-class university system integrated into a statewide education master plan, and many thousands of miles of interconnecting freeways. These were the building blocks that enabled the Golden State to become the world's ninth largest economy. Even as Google and Facebook thrive and the square footage of single-family homes has doubled, the public infrastructure has been left to crumble. The state's infrastructure deficit is estimated to be $765 billion.[21]

By 2011 these realities were so evident for all to see that *The Economist* devoted a cover story to the Golden State with this title: "Where It All Went Wrong: A Special Report on California's Dysfunctional Democracy."[22]

Surely, no system of governance can endure without the self-interested consent of the governed. Yet, neither can it endure, as every political sage from Plato to Madison understood, when ruled by the popular "appetite" (Plato's word).

Since the appetites and cultural habits of consumerism have so thoroughly infused all of America's institutions, clearly an evolution in democracy itself is required to temper its excesses with a new set of checks and balances. Institutionalized feedback arrangements that favor the long term and counter the ethos of immediate gratification are thus key to restoring good governance.

China Is Where California Was

All this contrasts sharply with America's top creditor, China, which is today investing heavily in its future the

34

way California and America did 50 years ago, building bullet trains that will link 80 percent of the population, expansive subway systems beneath its megacities, and a university system modeled on the Golden State's. China has also taken the lead in solar and many other renewable energy technologies, once the province of America's most environmentally sensitive state.

None of this is to say that China doesn't have serious problems or America doesn't have great strengths. It is to say that governance matters in whether a state or nation advances or regresses. And it does raise the issue of whether the fragmented and indebted consumer democracies of the West, hobbled by their short-term cultural habits and political horizons, are becoming ungovernable while the unified, far-sighted leadership of authoritarian China, despite immense challenges, is moving that country boldly and decisively into the future.

America is the borrower and consumer whose economy has become dominated by finance and services while inequality has grown dramatically. China is the investor and exporter whose economy is still industrializing, still largely impoverished, and sharply unequal.

This contrasting dynamic between two clashing systems has generated an imbalance in the global economy that, if not corrected, threatens the peace and prosperity that has so far been achieved through globalization. That correction cannot be economic alone, but depends as well on the recalibration of political systems in both West and East.

Sustained balance can be accomplished only by undoing the way American and Chinese inequalities have played off of each other – a low-wage export-led economy piling up huge reserves from overconsumption by an American middle class that fills the gap in its falling status through borrowing at rates pushed low by flush liquidity from China, abetted for years by accommodating Federal Reserve policies.* Good governance means being able to effect the transformation away from this state of affairs.

China's Modern Mandarinate

In China's case, a recalibration of the political system might mean a freer press to monitor government performance, supplementing the participatory power of that country's active webocracy, institutionalization of the rule of law through an independent judiciary, and broader electoral accountability to check the abuse of power by local political bosses, developers, or factory owners. With a one-party state and routine repression, China is certainly not an open society, and it still has a long way to go from rule-by-law to rule-of-law. But it is considerably more ajar than most in the West perceive.

A nation-wide welfare state, increased wages (including through more autonomous labor unions), and reform

---

* Richard Dobbs and Michael Spence have argued, however, that the "savings glut" was caused more by a decline in global investment, such as infrastructure and machinery, thus leading to a fall in demand for capital that was larger than the growth supply of China and other emerging economies (R. Dobbs and M. Spence, "The Era of Cheap Capital Draws to a Close," *Financial Times*, January 31, 2011).

As Martin Wolf reported, Mervyn King, Governor of the Bank of England, wrote in the February 2011 Financial Stability Review of the Banque de France that the "uphill flow" of capital from "poor to rich countries in supposedly safe assets had important consequences: a reduction of real interest rates; a rise in asset prices, particularly of housing in several countries, not least the US; a reach for yield; a wave of financial innovation to create higher yielding, but supposedly safe assets; a boom in residential construction; and, ultimately, a huge financial crisis" (M. Wolf, "Waiting for the Great Rebalancing," *Financial Times*, April 5, 2011).

36

of the *hukou* residency system so migrants can obtain urban services would further empower the household vis-à-vis the manufacturing sector, thus aiding the reorientation of China's juggernaut from export-led growth toward domestic consumption.

As Morgan Stanley's Stephen Roach[23] noted, China has a long way to go in building its safety net. He points out that, in 2009, the National Social Security Fund had only about $100 billion in assets under management, or about $110 per worker of life-time retirement benefits. Its 850 billion renminbi national healthcare plan translates into only $30 per capita over the coming years.

China might well learn from the policies of Asia's development pioneers – Japan, South Korea, or Taiwan – where income is more evenly spread as the result of the reliable rule of law, bargaining rights for unions, a credible safety net, and high and broad levels of investment in education and knowledge. A more even income spread and some sense of social security in a developing market like China would widely stimulate greater consumption.

Singapore's George Yeo is no doubt right for now when he says that China's "modern-day mandarinate" at the national level is largely meritocratic and geared to the common advance of the Chinese nation as a whole. However, the great challenge as China seeks to negotiate a middle-income transition like its modernized neighbors is whether the one-party mandarinate that has competently moved the Middle Kingdom from a peasant economy to the factory of the world will be able to transcend its Maoist roots and respond to the new conditions and constituencies it is creating. Samuel Huntington's famous thesis in *Political Order in Changing Societies*[24] was that turmoil, if not revolution, inevitably erupts when rising social aspirations are not met by evolving political institutions.

37

Unless it shifts its policies toward more openness and accountability and tends to the interests of the rising urban middle class while closing the inequality gap, China risks ending up in a stagnating cul-de-sac long before it reaches general prosperity. Though mum on political evolution, the country's 12th Five Year Plan charts precisely such a path, made more urgent by the fact that neither the US nor Europe, where growth has slowed as each deleverages its sovereign debt, can continue to play the role of China's consumer of last resort.

China is also urbanizing at a speed and on a scale never before seen in human history. In Mao's time, only 20 percent of the population lived in cities. Today it is 50 percent and will be 80 percent to 90 percent in the coming decades.

With more than a billion inhabitants, yet lacking less arable land than India and dependent on energy imports, China has embarked on a colossal effort to organize its immense population into efficient megacities with tens of millions of people. The McKinsey Global Institute[25] projects at least 15 such megacities with 25 million residents – each the population size of a major country.

Since the revolution concentrated land ownership in the hands of the state, the Chinese authorities have vast leeway in shaping these cities that must accommodate so many people, planning the urban infrastructure with high-speed connecting trains, state-of-the-art airports, deep subways, industrial parks, universities, and seas of skyscrapers.

"Although politics in China will change radically as the country urbanizes," says George Yeo, "the core principle of a bureaucratic elite holding the entire country together is not likely to change. Too many state functions affecting the well-being of the country as a whole require central coordination. In its historical memory, a China divided always means chaos."[26] Yet, without the civic software of enhanced accountability and transparency that complements the scale of their infrastructure hardware, will the Chinese bureaucratic elite be responsive enough to the needs, expectations, and aspirations of its burgeoning, ever more prosperous urban citizens? Can the same one-party system that focused single-mindedly on export-led growth also manage the diversifying interests of a more educated – and wired – population?

The sheer scale of China's challenges compels the leadership – obliged to pragmatically find solutions both by Confucian ethics and by the need to maintain the Communist Party's fragile legitimacy – to get up every morning and figure out how they are going to find jobs for the next 600 million people being added to the population in gigantic megacities that need everything from infrastructure to social welfare agencies to general practition doctors. "Social governance of the cities," Zheng Bijian, the powerful former vice-chair of the Central Party School, told us in a conversation in Beijing in June 2011, "is the preoccupation of the Party." Indeed, one does wonder how China would be able to meet these daunting challenges without a well-organized party that can chart a path forward and stick to it, albeit making adjustments as the facts dictate.

In their own ways, the city-states of Singapore and Hong Kong have shown China a path forward. While maintaining its strong meritocratic bias in governance, Singapore has loosened up considerably in recent years as a cosmopolitan hub of the global economy. Most importantly, its government consistently performs for the betterment of its citizens, vigilantly monitoring corruption, while keeping open channels of participation, even if short of robust multi-party competition. For the first time since it took power in 1965, in the May 2011 election, the ruling People's Action Party (PAP) founded by Lee Kuan Yew lost several key parliamentary seats to the opposition, spurring a further opening-up of the political system. Unlike in China, Singapore allows open political competition through social media.

Though part of China, Hong Kong has so far kept the rights of freedom of speech and assembly bequeathed by British rule while filtering direct popular rule through a legislative council that is partially apportioned to functional constituencies. This system falls short of the democratic aspirations of Hong Kongers – who want to move to universal suffrage by 2017 – yet it would be a big step forward if adopted by Beijing.

The Chinese mandarinate is already being tested on many fronts, from the need to stimulate domestic consumption as American and European demand for Chinese exports weakens, to endemic environmental crisis, to the striking workers at Honda, the 2009 suicides at the Foxconn factory that makes the iPod, and the widely reported village revolt in Wukan in 2011.

In some ways, the old guard of China's leadership – who still erroneously believe propaganda is possible in the glass house of the information age – are the mandarinate's worst enemy. The Chinese Communist Party's legitimacy is based upon performance, creating a kind of systemic accountability. Yet, when performance fails – such as after the Sichuan earthquake, when schools collapsed because of shoddy construction allowed through corrupt permit practices – the instinct is to cover the situation up instead of admit the problem and fix it, despite the true state of affairs being common knowledge. This is especially true today with the advent of *weibo* and the micro-blogging craze, which is China's version of Twitter. By May 2011, it had 230 million registered users. The more innovative among China's 457 million Netizens have become highly skilled at avoiding "harmonization" by the "automatic censors" that search for suspect words of political dissent. The resultant lack of trust among the public means many just don't believe any government information – even if it is true.

Although there are no elections above the village level in China, by all accounts most people have nonetheless granted their consent to the system because they believe it can deliver results. However, when the reality gap grows too large, when the distance between propaganda and truth is too great, one day people just stop believing in the system. Given a little push, it can fall. When you stretch the truth too far, it always breaks. This is what happened to the Soviet Union. In the advancing information age of the 21st century, the limits of propaganda are severely circumscribed.

For all their worries about China not suffering the fate of Soviet Union, the Party elders who try to spin reality to cover bad performance are making the same mistake the old Party ravens did in Moscow in the 1980s.

On a visit to Beijing's National Museum in June 2011, one could easily see the schizophrenia – or one could say lack of harmony – on display. In the North Wing of the Museum were splendid exhibits of classical landscape paintings by revered Chinese artists along with an exhibit from Germany on "The Age of Enlightenment." The walls were posted with large quotations about East learning from West and vice versa, including a quote from Schiller that "art is the daughter of freedom" – a thought not lost on anyone aware of Ai Weiwei's arrest and detention at that very time. In the "Path to Rejuvenation" exhibit at the other end of the museum devoted to the history of the Communist

41

Party, the explanatory plaques reverted to wooden propaganda. The Great Leap Forward and the Cultural Revolution, and the millions who suffered, were virtually erased by the censorious curators of history.

Clearly, some factions of the Chinese leadership are well aware of the need for accelerating democratic reform. Premier Wen Jiabao, who stepped down in a transfer of power in 2012, went further than any current leader when he said in an interview with CNN's Fareed Zakaria that "the people's wishes for and needs for democracy and freedom are irresistible." He also told Zakaria that "freedom of speech is indispensable for any country" and "that without the safeguard of political reform, the fruits of economic reform would be lost."[27] Wen repeated this sentiment in a remarkable press conference in March 2012 in Beijing at the close of the annual National People's Congress session. In that press conference, he also criticized Bo Xilai, the Chongqing Party chief, for his Maoist nostalgia and the use of an anti-corruption campaign to eliminate political enemies. The next day Bo Xilai was forced to step down.

The Communist Party secretary of Guangdong, Wang Yang, who, instead of cracking down, acceded to the demands of the Wukan villagers for fair compensation by land developers and appointed a protest leader as the local Party secretary there, has openly called for more democracy and fair elections in his province. By all accounts, the ouster of Bo Xilai, whose neo-Maoist vision was seen as competing with Wang's liberal tolerance, strengthened the hands of the more liberal elements in China's future.

What side of history the American or Chinese systems end up on will depend on governance. The United States remains paralyzed by an endless debate over how much government it wants and what its role is, though its political class remains ideologically rigid with respect to its commitment to liberal democracy as the best system ever invented by humanity. Chinese don't much question the economic or social role of the state but are instead engaged in intensive and wide-ranging debate over how much authoritarian meritocracy it needs versus how much democracy it can afford and still maintain "harmony" and stability. From the village level to the leadership compound of Zhongnanhai, discussions swirl, mostly privately but some publicly, over whether, and at what level, different models can be pragmatically accommodated. He Baogang, who has worked with the Central Party School on experiments in "deliberative democracy" at the village level in China, has characterized the present debate as a contention between the socialist model of one-party rule, the liberal democratic model of contending parties, and the Confucian model of no parties.[28]

A Debate between Francis Fukuyama and Zhang Weiwei on the Chinese Model

In a fascinating dialogue sponsored by the Chunqiu Institute in Shanghai in 2011, Francis Fukuyama[29] acknowledged the strengths of the Chinese system, pointed out its deep faults, and insisted on the superiority of liberal democracy as the best route to good governance. His dialogue partner, Zhang Weiwei, in turn extolled the virtues of China's system as more aligned with the future of humanity.

Fukuyama lauds China's "great historical achievement" of establishing the first state "that looked remarkably modern" during the Qin Dynasty 2,300 years ago in 221 BC. "The civil servants examination was invented in due course. You had a bureaucracy that was organized on rational lines and military forces in a large territory that were organized by unified rule." But, in Fukuyama's view, absent a dominant religion with moral rules to constrain the rulers, "China didn't develop the other two institutions [of the modern state]: rule of law and formal institutions of political accountability." Today, as then, according to Fukuyama, China's rulers are bound by "moral accountability" from the top to the bottom, which contrasts with "the procedural accountability of democratic elections." Today, "China is ruled by the Communist Party whose doctrine is Marxism, not Confucian ideology. But in many other respects the governance structure in China is very similar to the pattern established by the Qin Dynasty."[30]

Fukuyama then goes on to enumerate the strengths and weaknesses of the present "Chinese model" and contrast them with the strengths and weaknesses of liberal democracy.

First and foremost, China's decision-making processes are efficient because of its authoritarian capacity. If it wants to build the Three Gorges Dam, it has the resources not only to invest, but also to remove local populations that are in the way. By contrast, the US decision-making process is paralyzed by the partisan confrontation between Democrats and Republicans. Further,

> our interest groups are very powerful and capable of blocking some decisions. Although these decisions may be rational in the long term perspective, they are not taken in the end simply because of the opposition of some interest groups ... Whether we can change this state of affairs over the next few years is important in

judging whether the democratic system of the US can be
successful in the long run.[31]

Fukuyama doubts, however, whether China's model
will be sustainable over the coming decades because of
the lack of "downward accountability": "If you look at
the dynastic history in China you often see that a highly
centralized bureaucratic system with insufficient information and knowledge of the society results in ineffective governance. What bureaucracy brings is corruption
and bad governance. To some extent, this problem can
be observed in China today."[32]

The other issue of concern to Fukuyama is the "bad
emperor" problem:

> Undoubtedly if you have competent and well-trained
> bureaucrats, or well-educated technical professionals
> who are dedicated to the public interest, this kind of
> government is better than democratic government in the
> short term. Having a good emperor, however, doesn't
> guarantee that no bad emperor will emerge. There is
> no accountability system to remove the bad emperor if
> there is one. How can you get a good emperor? How can
> you make sure good emperors will reproduce themselves
> generation after generation? There is no ready answer.[33]

Zhang Weiwei argues, in turn, that, in many ways, the
Chinese model is more systemically accountable than
the US system. Chinese officials in the provinces, Zhang
notes, are tasked with promoting economic growth.
If they are successful, they are promoted. If not, they
are replaced by others who can do the job. As a result,
growth has been impressive across China for decades.

With respect to legal accountability, Zhang argues
that China easily stands up to the US. Citing a case in
Shanghai where a recent fire burned down a residential building, he notes that "twenty or so government

officials and corporate executives were arrested and punished for their negligence of duty and malpractice. In contrast, the financial crisis in the US has made American citizens lose one fifth to one quarter of their assets. Yet, three years have passed and nobody in the US has been held accountable politically, economically or legally."[34]

As for the "bad emperor" problem, Zhang believes the Chinese system is more self-correcting than the American system. Zhang points out that there have been at least seven dynasties in China, "during times of good and bad emperors," that each lasted more than 250 years, the entire history of the US with its slavery, lack of universal suffrage, and civil wars.

Zhang believes that China's "institutional innovation" has solved the issue since Mao:

> First and foremost, China's top leadership is selected on merits, not heredity. Second, the term of office is strict and top leaders serve a maximum of two terms. Third, collective leadership is practiced, which means no single leader can prevail if he deviates too much from the group consensus. Last, but not least, meritocracy-based selection is a time-honored tradition in China, and top-level decision makers are members of the Standing Committee of the Politburo who are selected with criteria that usually requires two terms as provincials governors of ministers. . . . [P]rovinces in China are the size of four or five European countries.[35]

Because of this culture of "talent first" that stems populism, mob rule, or "rule by anyone who is elected," Zhang believes a meritocracy on the lines of China's model, which combines election and selection, is more likely to be sustainable than liberal democracy, which, in his view, "might be only transitory in the long history of mankind."[36]

46

For his part, Fukuyama believes that the process of modernization will ultimately cause China, like other East Asia societies rooted in Confucianism, such as Japan and Taiwan, to accept "upward accountability" in the form of democratic electoral accountability. While for Fukuyama, "middle class people in different cultures actually believe in a similar way," Zhang's belief is that the idea that "modernization leads to cultural convergence" is a figment of Western hubris of the "end of history" variety.[37]

Zhang's position is the same as Sam Huntington,[38] of the "clash of civilizations" fame, who believed the process of modernization would be adapted in different ways by different civilizations and would not amount to "Westernization." Interestingly, both Fukuyama and Fareed Zakaria, who agrees with Fukuyama, were Huntington's students at Harvard.

Our approach in this book agrees with Zhang and Huntington that modernization need not be "Western" and that China must adopt a more robust system of accountability from within its political and cultural traditions. We also agree with what Zhang suggests: without deep structural reforms that rival what China must do, democracy as it concretely exists in America today is not so self-correcting as Fukuyama believes.

To explore just what those reforms might be, we revisit some of the past debates over political meritocracy versus democracy in this new context.

3

Liberal Democratic Constitutionalism and Meritocracy

Hybrid Possibilities

Introduction

The debate over meritocracy versus democracy is, of course, not new. In the West it goes back to Plato's vision of governance as the rule of the few guided by trained reason in pursuit of the ideal and has continued to modern theorists such as John Rawls,[1] who doubted that a just society could be sustained when the uninformed individual voter acts in his or her own self-interest instead of the common interest.

In their design of republican government, James Madison and the other American Founding Fathers influenced by the ideas of the Enlightenment worried about too much democracy and sought to check the tyranny of the majority and the immediate passions of men with institutions like the electoral college, the deliberative Senate, and non-elected bodies like the Supreme Court. They also believed that the good society should be ruled by a learned elite not unlike themselves.

As the great University of Chicago sinologist H.G. Creel has suggested, Thomas Jefferson very much came

48

to admire Confucian ideas through his reading of Voltaire, who declared in the 1770s "that the mind of man could not imagine a better government than China where virtually all power lay in the hands of bureaucrats whose members were admitted only after several severe examinations."[2] Government by virtuous and talented men whose position in life was due to merit, not heredity, perfectly fit Jefferson's republican vision of constitutional government rooted in popular sovereignty but ruled by neither monarch nor mob.

Creel cites Jefferson's natural affinity with the Confucian worldview in an 1813 letter to John Adams:

> I agree with you that there is a natural aristocracy among men. The grounds of this are virtue and talents. . . . There is also an artificial aristocracy, founded on wealth and birth. . . . The natural aristocracy I consider as the most precious gift of nature, for the instruction, the trusts, and government of society. . . . May we not even say, that the form of government is the best, which provides most effectually for a pure selection of these natural aristoi in the offices of government.[3]

As Creel notes after quoting this passage, "It would be difficult to epitomize the theory of the Chinese examination system more neatly." Indeed, Jefferson had proposed legislation in 1779 for education at the public expense with a stepped examination system from grade school to William and Mary College "for the selection of youths of genius from among the classes of the poor . . . to avail the state of those talents which nature has sown as liberally among the poor as the rich."[4]

Although there may be scant evidence of the direct influence of Confucian precepts on Jefferson other than the extensive notations in his copy of Voltaire's book that discusses China, there is little doubt of that influence among the intellectuals of the Enlightenment at the time.

Creel cites the historian Adolf Reichwein that the philosophers of the Enlightenment "discovered, to their astonishment, that more than two thousand years ago in China ... Confucius had thought the same thoughts in the same manner, and fought the same battles.... Confucius became the patron saint of the 18th-century Enlightenment."[5] The nobility of reason in the name of a harmonious and just society was no less their cause than it was that of the ancient sage. Though later wary of the decay into despotism of the Confucian ideal, Montesquieu wrote that "the emperor of China ... knows that if his empire be not just, he will be stript both of empire and life.... This empire is formed on the plan of a government of [all as] a family."[6] Extolling its meritocratic qualities, the Jesuit Louis-Daniel Le Comte published an article in Paris in 1696, saying that, in China, "nobility is never hereditary, neither is there any distinction between the qualities of people; saving what the offices which they execute makes."[7] Mostly informed, like others, about China by the scholarly Jesuit missionaries under Matteo Ricci, Gottfried Leibniz wrote:

> Even if we are equal to them in the productive arts, and if we surpass them in the theoretical sciences, it is certainly true (and I am almost ashamed to admit) that they surpass us in practical philosophy, by which I mean the rules of ethics and politics which have been devised for the conduct and benefit of human life.[8]

In China, the idea of "elevating the worthy" to positions of power despite pedigree can be traced back to the Warring States period of 453–221 BC.[9] Selecting "virtuous and talented" government officials became a systematic practice during the Western Han dynasty (202 BC–9 AD). Examinations for talent were added to screening in the Eastern Han period (25–220 AD).[10]

Strong traces of this "institutional civilization" are found today in the "promotion through competition" practice of the modern mandarinate of the Communist Party, which seeks to ferret out the best civil servants and move them up through the ranks. In China, there is no way someone like President Barack Obama could win two non-national elections (to the Illinois State Senate then to the US Senate) and move to the top post of president without any prior testing in an executive position. China's Xi Jinping, who (at time of writing) is expected to become the country's new president and general secretary, was governor or Party secretary of several provinces – Fujian, Zhejiang, and Shanghai – before becoming vice-president.

Considering the tradeoffs between democracy and meritocracy or the idea of blending their qualities in a hybrid system has once again become a hot topic, not only because of the demonstrable success of China's modern mandarinate in delivering hundreds of millions from the scourge of poverty in a mere 30 years, but also because of the generalized crisis of governance across the Western democracies today.

Conventional wisdom no doubt rightly holds that as China moves away from the investment–export model of growth – which is more prone to guidance by a talented political class – and toward a middle-class transition, it will have to evolve more democratic elements of feedback and accountability.

At the same time, in response to the paralysis of partisan politics engendered by electoral democracy in the West, the idea of depoliticized meritocracy as a key element of restoring good governance is already being tested. One example is the so-called "supercommittee" of the US Congress, convened as a nonpartisan means "beyond politics" to cut America's long-term fiscal deficits. The most prominent example, however, has been the installation of Mario Monti's unelected "technocratic government" in Italy.

Because elected politicians couldn't get their act together, Monti was appointed by President Giorgio Napolitano late in 2011[11] to formulate and implement key structural reforms until new elections are called in 2013.

Italy got into its mess not because of too little democracy, but because of too much decay in its form of governance. Italian electoral democracy – like that in the US – is so politicized along partisan lines that it became dysfunctional and wholly incapable of meeting the tough challenges facing the country.

Monti, whose fair-minded wisdom and long experience as a European commissioner make him more a meritocrat than a technocrat, was certainly right to declare that "the absence of political personalities in the government would help rather than hinder a solid base of support"[12] for reform.

He understood that Italian democracy, like American democracy, has become a "vetocracy," to use a phrase coined by Francis Fukuyama that we noted earlier. In a vetocracy, elected politicians are so captured by short-term populist sentiment and organized special interests that the mere formulation of a policy that seeks compromise for the long-term common good is eviscerated by the parties in play even before it can be put to a vote in Parliament. Any bill that gets through is so shorn of substance as to be meaningless. So what remains is the status quo.

In *The Rise and Decline of Nations*,[13] as we also

previously noted, the social scientist Mancur Olson described how this powerful accretion of organized interests in democracies over time has dragged down states time and again because it inevitably produces unsustainable deficits and drains an economy of vigor by protecting "rent-seeking" cartels.

If left up to elected officials, parties representing taxi driver unions or pharmacists weren't about to favor making their clients' lives more difficult through open competition. Public employees resisted cuts in jobs and benefits. Bankers used their influence with legislators to avoid regulation. The rich sought to block higher taxes. Giving voters a bigger say through direct instead of representative democracy couldn't be the answer, either. If put to a popular vote, what pensioner would be in favor of trimming the generous social contract he or she has come to expect, even if the collective Italian purse can't afford it?

We saw in the previous chapter how in California, where the direct democracy of the initiative process dominates governance, rational self-interest expressed by voters at the ballot box can add up to unintended consequences for the whole public. We also noted there how, absurdly, the state spends more on prisons than on higher education. In Chapter 6 we will discuss in more detail how this state of affairs resulted from a series of initiatives over the years slashing property taxes while seeking to get tough on crime.

As difficult to swallow as his dose of discipline was, the depoliticized democracy practiced by Prime Minister Monti was the only possible form of government that could move Italy forward. And we will see more and more of it in the West for the same reasons as we've seen in Italy.

No one, least of all the present authors, is suggesting

doing away with one-person-one-vote democracy and transferring popular sovereignty to a meritocratic elite, as is the case, for example, with the Communist Party mandarinate in China. For the West, the ultimate say must reside with the voting public who consent to their form of governance. But stripping out the "vetocracy" aspect of policy-making is key to good governance. Instead of only pulling the lever out of narrow self-interest or being called upon to sift through the thicket of spin and special interests at election time, the public should be able to decide on considered policies proposed to them by bodies entrusted to take into account the long-term common interest.

The current travails of governance in the West suggest that an evolution of democracy is necessary in which institutions with meritocratic elements are established as a way to counterbalance the short-term, special-interest political culture of electoral democracy.

Italy's experiment with depoliticized democracy will be closely watched as an antidote to the paralysis and dysfunction that afflicts the West today. If political decay can yield to good governance in Italy, everyone will have benefited from the path blazed by Mario Monti.

As "depoliticized spaces," deliberative institutions require a certain opacity to shield their decisions from popular pressure and the "tyranny of the majority." This is why the US Supreme Court and the Federal Reserve are not "transparent" institutions. Opacity allows the breathing space for reasoned deliberation not subject to popular opinion.

However, to ensure that deliberative institutions don't become hidebound, they must be linked to robust feedback loops and replenished or "aerated" periodically, both by having to argue publicly for the legitimacy of their decisions and through rotations of personnel. One need only look to the old Soviet *nomenklatura* or the Japanese nuclear bureaucracy to make this point.

In order to sort out which qualities of democracy and meritocracy are most useful to good governance today, it will be helpful to look at the origins of China's "institutional civilization" as well as the early arguments of the American Founding Fathers about the republican virtues of *government for the people* in a constitutional democracy versus mass electoral participation in *government by the people*.

China's "Institutional Civilization"

Pan Wei, who has studied the meritocratic practices of the Communist Party, has usefully offered a framework that distinguishes Eastern and Western approaches to governance.[14]

Pan argues that all governance of human affairs involves a mix of four approaches: adjudication (rule of law), accountability, responsibility, and justice. "Because of China's traditional social structure," he contends, "governance in China has historically relied more upon responsibility and justice than on adjudication and accountability."

While European societies had clear and stable divisions, Pan argues "it was impossible to find a 'stable ruling class' in China between the fourth century BC and the beginning of the 20th century." For those millennia Chinese society was like "a heap of sand," consisting of independent, small-scale family farms of roughly equal size. This "undifferentiated" peasant heap led, in Pan's view, to the holistic concept of "all families." While large gaps between rich and poor existed, the lack of primogeniture meant a certain fluid mobility since "no rich family could sustain for more than three generations."

The major rebellions that overthrew dynasties were general "peasant rebellions" against the rulers of a particular dynasty, not class revolts of the poor against the rich, and the country always reverted to the same social system afterward.

This reality, according to Pan, fundamentally shaped the evolution of governance in China. Rather than the emergence of a legalistic "social contract" among individuals and classes, a mutually obligatory "moral economy" of subsistence agriculture dominated. "Lawmaking is not a core issue in Chinese political life," Pan says. Further, because of this holistic conception of society, legitimacy of governance was related to accountability to the whole society, not to partial interests, or parties. "Party competition unavoidably leads to selfish purposes."

It was from within this social context that China's "institutional civilization," or *min-ben* polity, arose as an ideal, with its emphasis on ethical government for "the welfare of all families" (the common good) run by virtuous and talented civil servants based on a moral obligation of the rulers to the ruled. *Min-ben* means "rooted in the people."

According to Pan, the *min-ben* system took hold more than 3,000 years ago in the Western Zhou Dynasty, was elaborated by Confucius centuries later, and was the basis of the competitive examination mandarinate for 1,700 years until the beginning of the 20th century.

Though patronage and connections have contaminated this ideal system like all others, it is above all the principle of examination and promotion through performance evaluation that defines China's "institutional civilization."

"It is meritocracy that makes the Chinese polity different from electoral democracy. The meritocratic principle based on competition holds the same central position in the history of Chinese governance as the electoral principle of the majority holds in electoral democracy," Pan told us when we met in Beijing.

Other key aspects of China's ethical system of governance, which, according to Pan, existed from the Qin Dynasty (221–206 BC) through the Qing Dynasty (1644–1911), are the concept of the "Grand Unity" of the whole society, which has been embedded in the mindset of Chinese since the first Emperor Qin, as well as the mistake-correction mechanism of "supervisory institutions" that check the "unified governing group" through a "division of labor" instead of a separation of powers.

These features are evident in China today under Communist Party rule. Since Mao's deviant idea of "class struggle" was jettisoned under Deng Xiaoping's modernization, the Party today claims to represent "all of society" and seeks "harmony." Multi-party political competition is rejected as lacking legitimacy because it would fragment the "Grand Unity" in the name of "partial" or "special interests."

If in less than ideal form and practice, "mistake-correction" supervisory institutions exist in China and elsewhere in the Confucian-influenced polities. With its independent inspection commission, Singapore has effectively rooted out corruption in government. Such disciplinary institutions exist in China as well but are more or less effective depending on the political will at the local or national level.

The vast use of *weibo* is one way for the common

57

person to supervise and challenge the government along with the formal right to petition government over abuses, which unfortunately too often leads to harassment and intimidation in turn. China's *de facto* federalism sets up a system where the provinces and Beijing check and balance each other. The four-level National People's Congress and the three-level Consultative Council can have real impact, depending on the issue. Finally, as Pan sees it, there is the check and balance between Party and state, which do not always see eye to eye. He distinguishes between the Soviet Union, where the state was built for the party – a "party state" – and the "state party" in China, where, echoing the Confucian past, the Party certifies the meritocratic personnel for state power.

The Founding Fathers

The American republic, to this day having existed only for a briefer period than most Chinese dynasties, had quite different origins. It was designed at the outset to curb the power of government and to maximize the freedom of propertied individuals and the religious conscience. While the Antifederalists favored more direct democracy and worried about giving too much power to representative elites distant from the people, the Federalists sought to delegate authority to institutions such as the electoral college, the Senate, the Supreme Court, and later a central bank, where the meritorious would be empowered to serve the public. The Federalists sought to temper pure expressions of popular will so that liberty was no more threatened by the irrational tyranny of the majority than by a singular monarch. Rather than expect a unified governing class as the Chinese ancients did, the American founders sought as well to design ways to check the natural emergence of "factions"[15] through a "separation of powers" that would prevent capture of the commonweal by partial, or special, interests. In a federal arrangement, the power of the center was also circumscribed by broad autonomy of the states.

As the Princeton political scientist Stephen Macedo[16] has written, the experience of popular self-rule under the Articles of Confederation from 1781 to 1789 gave rise to concerns among the Federalist-oriented that "institutions too responsive to the public – with short terms of office – would tend to be fickle, unwise and irresponsible." The Framers of the American Constitution did not favor "democracy," which they understood in terms of direct democracy with a strong tendency toward instability, lack of wisdom, and majority tyranny. But they endorsed the republican principle according to which all political authority was understood to flow from the people. In Federalist Paper No. 10, Madison in particular emphasized that the biggest difference between the new American polity and Ancient Greek democracy was "the total exclusion of the people in their collective capacity" from government.

As Macedo points out, the public's formal direct power under the Constitution consisted of electing representatives to the lower house of the national legislature. To balance this popular voice, neither the Senate nor the Supreme Court was selected or accountable in direct popular elections. (Until the early 20th century, the US Senate was chosen by state legislatures.)

The argument by Madison[17] in Federalist Paper No. 62 against a directly elected Senate, according to Macedo, was that it should represent "the cool and deliberate sense of the community" against "the temporary errors and delusions" of the people's own immediate representatives in the lower house. "How salutary," wrote Madison, "will be the interference of some temperate and respectable body of citizens in order to check [ill-conceived proposals] until reason, justice and truth can regain their authority over the public mind."

Further, in the original design, even the strong executive of the presidency was not popularly elected, but selected by an "electoral college" also chosen by the state legislatures. The idea, as spelled out in Federalist Paper No. 68, was to "refine and enlarge the public views by passing them through the medium of a chosen body of citizens."[18]

These early debates about how to reconcile meritocratic authority with popular sovereignty resonate very clearly today as short-term populist passions and partisan strife have paralyzed American governance at a time when it is not facing down a distant monarch across the Atlantic but facing the challenges and opportunities of the powerful re-emergence of China's "institutional civilization" across the Pacific.

As Macedo[19] correctly argues, it is time for America to return to "a mixed constitutional conception of democracy" that incorporates the values associated with meritocracy along with consent of the governed. "I reject the tendency to flatten and simplify the democratic landscape, placing tremendous emphasis on popular elections and the elected representative. When mass publics contemplate constitutional design, they recognize that a richer and more complex set of institutional arrangements are needed to realize in practice the values of self-government by all in the name of all."

Meritocratic institutions with delegated authority, after all, are not foreign to democracies and, as we've discussed, were clearly in the minds of the Founding

Fathers in the United States. The US has an independent central bank, higher courts, and powerful regulatory bodies in areas ranging from food and drugs to the environment and health. Even in California's radical democracy, key powers have been granted to commissions appointed by the governor that regulate development along the coast, oversee the state's energy and water supply, and administer the University of California. All are accountable to the public because they are appointed by democratically elected officials, yet they are all insulated from the electoral process itself.

In this brief summary we can easily see that the same issues of governance concerned both the ancient sages of China and the American Founding Fathers despite their vastly different cultural and historical settings. In the next section we will explore the institutional design of a hybrid, "mixed constitutional" template of "intelligent governance" that seeks to incorporate the proven best practices of each – competent government guided by cool deliberation and talent married to the self-correcting qualities of democratic feedback and accountability.

Hybrid Systems with a Mixed Constitution

As we have shown, there is much history under the bridge of today's interdependence between China and the West, going back centuries, that inhibits convergence of political thought. China's ancient "Warring States Period" ended with a commitment to unified territorial integrity and stability that led to a modern focus on political control and social harmony. The path to peace after the West's religious wars in the Middle Ages led to the opposite ideals: tolerance and diversity. In the Confucian tradition, China has relied on ethics and education of elites to keep its institutions responsive, fair, and honest. The West has relied on the check of multi-party democracy and the rule of law.

Yet, as suggested by Thomas Jefferson's admiration of Confucius, noted above, there are even deeper strands of the humanist tradition in both the East and the West that stretch back millennia.

Michael Lind, a senior fellow at the New America Foundation, has pointed out that both China and the West share a tradition of "classical humanism – a cultural pattern that flourished in ancient China, ancient Greece and Rome as well as in the Renaissance and Baroque eras."[20]

For Lind, all these classical humanists shared

> a focus on human life combined with a high degree of indifference to supernatural and metaphysical questions; an emphasis on practical reason or common sense; deductive rationalism or individual genius and respect for a classical literary tradition embodying the wisdom of the past. Confucius, Sun-tze, Socrates, Aristotle, Cicero, Erasmus and Voltaire, brought back to life, would share a great deal in common with one another.[21]

In his 2011 book, *On China*, Henry Kissinger echoes Lind's observation. "China owed its millennial survival far less to the punishment meted out by its Emperors than to the community of values fostered among its population and its government of scholar-officials," he writes. "Not the least exceptional aspect of Chinese culture is that these values were essentially secular in nature. . . . Spiritual fulfillment was a task not so much of revelation or liberation but patient recovery of forgotten principles of self-restraint."[22]

Though Lind worries that a belief in "the 'science' of government and the idea of non-partisan technocracy"[23]

– owing to the influence of Western utilitarianism and the ideological remnants of Marxism in China – risks eclipsing a revival of the practical reason of classical humanism based on perennial wisdom, the growing interdependence between China and the US also offers the chance for a new synthesis.*

"There was no Central Asian philosopher to effect a synthesis of Mediterranean and Asian humanism in 1200 A.D.," Lind writes. "But today, when religion has been dislodged from control of intellectual life, and when the Romantic and rationalist utopias alike have failed, there is an opportunity to weave together what is best and most enduring in Hellenic and Sino-Asian humanism to provide a 'usable past'" for the new global civilization.[24]

Ironically, as the Chinese entrepreneur and scholar Eric X. Li has observed, China and the West, particularly America, have gone in opposite directions in this respect since the end of the Cold War. Just as China was leaving its ideology behind and returning to its "seek truth from facts" Confucian roots, the once pragmatic Americans have reified their version of democracy into an ideology. Li writes:

> Tactically on the winning side of the Cold War, China nevertheless saw the worldwide collapse of the communist ideology it embraced since the founding of the People's Republic. As the Chinese Communist Party

---

* An interesting contrast on this front could be seen in the different approaches to politics in California. Former Speaker of the Assembly and San Francisco mayor Willie Brown's approach to politics has been to build a network of promising young politically oriented people whom he mentors through ever higher posts toward executive power. Eric Schmidt of Google's approach to ending partisan gerrymandering of districts is to divide the state in parallelogram grids by formula, thus removing the role of politics in designing districts.

maintained its grip on power and led China in a dramatic ascendancy in all aspects of national power, the country has turned its back on communist ideology. In fact, it has turned its back on ideology itself, which was a Western import to begin with.[25]

Finding literally bronze-cast proof of China's return to its non-ideological civilization roots would require looking no further than the National Museum in the heart of Beijing. In a part of the capital where everything is highly symbolic, a nine-meter-high statue of Confucius was erected in January 2011. At first, it was placed right on Chang'an Avenue in front of the Museum just across from Mao's portrait hanging over the gate to the Forbidden City and next to the Great Leader's mausoleum. The Western press speculated that, perhaps as an illustration of the lingering sensitivities of the so-called "Maoist conservatives" who identify the Confucian order with feudalism, the statue was moved in April of that year to an interior courtyard. Other evidence, such as a review of the raging *weibo* debate on the subject, suggests many Chinese thought it was just bad *feng shui*. In any case, the imposing statue is now still plainly visible to museum-goers, if not by passers-by.

This whole episode, along with the official establishment of Confucius Institutes around the world, reflects nonetheless that China's leaders as well as civil society, such as it is, are engaged in a broad consideration of China's identity as a re-emergent "civilizational state" and what reform possibilities the end of ideology might open up.

As Eric X. Li has put it unsentimentally:

Western democracy is inherently incapable of becoming less democratic even when its survival may depend on such a shift. The Chinese, on the other hand, would allow greater popular participation in political decisions when it is conducive to economic development and favorable to its national interests, as they have done in the past 10 years, but would not hesitate to curtail it if the conditions and the needs of the nation change.[26]

For America, democracy is an end in itself. In the post-ideological pragmatism proposed by Chinese thinkers such as Eric X. Li or Zhang Weiwei,[27] democracy is only a means to the end of good governance. "If it helps deliver results, great. If not, who needs it?" is their view.

Counterintuitive as it may appear to the Western mindset, China in many ways is more open to fundamental political reform than is the US. Since the US system is based upon the notion that the state itself is constrained by a body of pre-existing law that is sovereign, any thought of rewriting the Constitution is nearly anathema.

In China, however, some intellectuals point out that the remnants of Communist Party theory posit that the current system is the "primary stage of socialism," meaning that it is a transitional phase to a higher and more superior form of socialism. The economic foundation will change with broader prosperity, and thus the legal and political superstructure must also change.

That has led some contemporary Confucian scholars in China to argue that Marxism cannot be the philosophy of the higher stage of development, not least since it is a foreign ideology, and that any new form of government must be based on indigenous sources of legitimacy from within the Chinese experience – meritocratic knowledge of the governing class, the ethical obligation of the ruler to the ruled, and tradition.

Daniel A. Bell, a Canadian scholar who teaches comparative political philosophy at Tsinghua University in Beijing, is one who believes the current moment in which a Confucian renaissance meets China's middle-class transition, with all the pressure that brings to bear for more participation and accountability, is ripe for reform.[28]

Bell envisions a meritocratic upper house whose members are chosen not by election but by competitive examination, or *Xianshiyuan*; an elected national democratic legislature that advises the upper house on "preferences"; direct elections up to the provincial level; and freedom of the press. The head of state and top ministers would be chosen from among the most august members of the meritocratic house. Bell would give the upper hand to the upper house, which could override a majority vote in the lower house with a supermajority vote.

After the Egyptian Facebook revolution, many Western commentators naïvely predicted that a virtual Tiananmen Square uprising would sooner or later hit China's autocratic rulers like it had hit Mubarak, ending in the very real occupation of Tahrir Square. Bell argued in February 2011 that even among Chinese intellectuals there was a clear attitude that "democracy is not so good." He divided these intellectuals into "pessimists" and "optimists." The pessimists felt that democracy would give vent to racism, national fascism, and irrational mob rule, as during the Cultural Revolution. Yet even the optimists, who want more accountability to curb corruption in the Party and make it more responsive to urban consumer constituencies, nonetheless don't want multi-party elections or direct elections for the top leaders.

In Bell's view, they would prefer that decisions concerning land disputes, for example, in rural China, take place in a democratic legislature while longer-term and global concerns like the environment and foreign policy be taken up by a meritocratic house.

On the larger recalibration of the political system, Bell wrote, "Democrats often respond with an objection that democracy is a priority: Let's democratize the system first, and then we can think about how to improve democracy."

But multi-party elections for the top leaders, Bell argued, would take China back down the path of what ails the West. "The current political system in China is already meritocratic in some respects," he noted, "and it would be practical and desirable to draw on the parts that work well." He went on to say:

> Cadres in the 78 million strong Chinese Communist Party are increasingly selected according to competitive meritocratic criteria. And the government implements some policies according to five-year plans that are designed for long-term benefit, such as support for clean energy, high-speed railways and economic development projects in the sparsely populated western part of the country. A more democratic government would be more constrained by short-term electoral considerations.

Such a formulation and others similar to it – about which there is a rich debate across China today – stick to the Confucian idea of an excellent meritocratic government mitigated by popular accountability but not completely ruled by it. This seems precisely the kind of non-Western political modernization we will see as China adopts its own form of democratization.

Even key Party figures in China believe that more accountability is desperately needed to stem the arbitrariness, corruption, and cronyism that have accompanied the primary stage of socialism. All too easily the strong hand of the state can become the harsh fist of repression or the open palm of corruption.

Yet such an approach as put forth by Bell is likely to also maintain stability in a way that electoral democracy of the West might not, and thus would be a realistic and viable course of change in China.

While Bell's proposal seeks to democratize China's modern mandarinate along Confucian lines, the Fudan University political philosopher Bai Tongdong wants to Confucianize democracy to correct its faults. Bai believes that "an ideal Confucian form of governance"[29] would remove the chief impediments to good governance posed by one-person-one-vote democracy that have been most thoroughly pondered by John Rawls in *Political Liberalism*.[30]

As Bai reads him, Rawls first of all points out that the one-person-one-vote system encourages the tendency of individuals to fall back on self-interest when considering public issues. Second, many citizens indifferently abstain from elections. Third, modern democracies are so large and complex, and people's lives are so busy with work and family, that the average citizen lacks the knowledge to make informed decisions. Fourth, with so many voters owing to universal suffrage, individual votes are virtually meaningless. Fifth, the power of money in politics, especially from the largest special interests such as corporations, distorts honest discourse and undermines the utility of elections as means of promoting the common good. (And this was well before the US Supreme Court ruling that sanctioned money as "free speech" in political campaigns.)

Firmly ensconced in Western political thought, what seems to be Rawls' chief remedy for the flaws of electoral democracy is not to delegate authority to the more knowledgeable, as the experience of China's "institutional civilization" would suggest, but to improve the knowledge of citizens to act responsibly through "deliberative democracy." This remedy seeks to reconcile the fact that, as one scholarly wag has put it, "deliberative citizens do not participate much, and participatory citizens do not deliberate much,"[31] with the belief of Justice Louis Brandeis that "in a democracy, the most important office is the office of the citizen."[32]

Following Rawls, the deliberative experiment has been tried here and there across the West – albeit as an advisory, not a binding element of governance – in Canada, Australia, and California.

The earliest practice of deliberative democracy through indicative representation can be traced to ancient Greece, with its "random sampling" lottery system to choose the general assemblies. The American jury system draws on this tradition. But the most cited case so far of modern deliberative democracy as a form of democratic representation is the Citizens' Assembly that was convened in the Canadian province of British Columbia in 2004 to review the extant election system, host a series of hearings and discussions, and recommend reforms. Those reforms were put forward to a vote in a public referendum, though they fell just short of the required majority at the polls.[33]

In California, as we will discuss in greater detail in Chapter 6, we tried a similar tack of "indicative representation" by establishing an independent bipartisan group in 2011 called the Think Long Committee, with self-selected members ranging from Google's Eric Schmidt to the former chief justice of the state's Supreme Court to former US Secretary of State Condoleezza Rice. It left politics aside and was able to reach a bipartisan tax-reform plan bridging the ideological divide that has paralyzed the state legislature for years. It will offer that plan to the public for a vote in a ballot initiative in 2014. The group has further proposed a more formal nonpartisan body, appointed by elected officials but composed of prominent citizens with expertise and experience, to watch over California's long-term interests.

Parallel to this process, the Think Long Committee joined with another reform group, California Forward, to sponsor a weekend-long "deliberative poll" in which a random sample of citizens was called together to identify the key reforms they thought would remedy California's dysfunctional state government. The ideas they generated – a "pay-go" requirement that the legislature specify either the cuts or revenues that would compensate for new spending, two-year performance-based budgeting, and more transparency and oversight to government operations – were incorporated into an initiative that was successfully put before the voters as a ballot initiative in 2012.

Deliberative democracy strays from the assumption that the electorate at large will choose the best leaders and creates instead the opportunity for voters to choose the best policies that have been deliberatively considered. In short, it is a kind of half-way measure that shifts the burden of knowledge in governance from the average voter to the deliberating "indicative" voter. It does not delegate authority for governance to the most meritorious.

Professor Bai's "ideal Confucian form of government," which he believes offers a more systemic response to Rawls' flaws than the indirect influence on power of deliberative democracy, would go this further distance.[34]

Bai contends that "the Confucian would be in favor of a hybrid system that would introduce and strengthen the role of the competent and moral 'meritocrats' along with the institution of one-person-one-vote." Such a hybrid system, in Bai's view, would both conform more closely to Confucian principles than China's current system and enhance democracy by improving "government for the people, but not entirely by the people." The foundations of what Bai calls "Confu-China" are the rule of law, human rights, and the containment of social inequality, following Rawls' "difference principle." Not only should education in general, including civic education, be the basis of the right to participate in politics, guaranteed by freedom of speech, but that participation ought to be meaningful on a scale that enables "civic friendship" in the management of common affairs and not just, as in the larger Western democracies like the US, the formal, mostly meaningless right to vote.

Bai's concept rests on a leveled system that combines election at the grass-roots level and selection of the "experienced and learned" at higher levels in order to achieve both legitimacy and competence.

While the right of citizens to have their full say should be respected at the local level where they live and work – or when larger issues affect their local well-being – citizens in turn must respect "the competent and virtuous that run the government" at a higher level.

Though defining what "local" means is an empirical question, Bai's principle is this: "How much democratic participation should depend on how likely the participants are able to make sound decisions that are based upon the public interest."

On issues that arise at levels beyond the local community where citizens are "indifferent, or they lack the capacity to make sound judgments," then arrangements should be made "to limit the influence of popular will on policies."

For Bai, the capacity for sound judgment by voters could certainly be enhanced by increasing their knowledge through deliberative convocations on certain policies, or, more controversially, weighting the votes of those who demonstrably understand the issues. But Bai's system would go further by establishing a leveled or stepped system where more competence is required the higher up the decision-making ladder one goes, culminating, like Daniel Bell's proposal, in a bicameral system where an unelected "upper house" of the learned balances an elected "lower house" that begins with one-person-one-vote popular representation at the grass roots but from that level up chooses officials "through internal election, selection or recommendation" based on experience. The experienced capable of higher affairs could be selected by the local electorate based on the demonstrated capabilities in local affairs, the experience they have gained through interface with higher levels of governance, or their experience gained as industry leaders, scientists, or non-governmental activists.

Bai hastens to point out that his proposed model is "different from representative democracy in that the local officials who enter higher-level government are not representatives of local interests, but are those who are capable of participating in policy-making on a higher level."

The members of Bai's learned "upper house," as in Bell's proposal, would be chosen by competitive examination not unlike the old *keju* system, "where the literati obtained titles of different levels which may lead to different positions in government by passing further exams on corresponding levels." Performance recommendation – not unlike the way the Organization Department of today's Communist Party functions – would be another basis for selecting the members of the meritocratic upper house.

Both the proposals by Bell and Bai amend Sun Yat-sen's effort to combine Confucianism and democracy in his famous "five branch" government, weakly echoed in Taiwan today, which added an "Examination *Yuan*" and a "Control *Yuan*" to contain corruption within the legislative, executive, and judicial *yuans*, or branches. In a way, Bell and Bai are more politically viable, both because the Confucian foundations of China's "institutional civilization" are experiencing a renaissance today, whereas they were tainted by the decadent despotism of the late imperial dynasty at the turn of the 20th century, and because the crisis of governance in the West has so well revealed the flaws of one-person-one-vote democracy.

Remarkably, while we added to Rawls' flaws to be corrected the crippling short-termism of consumer democracies, Bai's design is very close to the design we came up with after convening a months-long discussion of Western scholars in Los Angeles in 2010.

Like Bai, we agreed that the foundations of any legitimate system of governance must be to contain too much social inequality while ensuring free expression and the rule of law. Clearly, the ability of any system, whether meritocratic or democratic, to self-correct depends more on an "open society" than on one-person-one-vote elections. As Bai has put it, "the gems of liberal democracy are rights and the rule of law, not elections." Then, like Bai, we envisioned a leveled system starting with elected government at the grass roots that chooses higher-level officials based on competence up to the level of a "lower house," all to be checked further with an unelected "upper house" of the "wise, expert, and experienced" to balance the short-term, self-interested nature of the lower house.

As an act of political imagination, in Chapter 5

we flesh out in greater detail the institutional design of a mixed constitutional system that combines and seeks to balance both the elements of meritocracy and democracy.

First, however, we must take a quick detour of the newest challenges to good governance in the 21st century that bear on the design of new institutions – the emergence of social media networks, the rise of megacities and the global scattering of production.

4

The New Challenges for Governance

Social Networks, Megacities, and the Global
Scattering of Productive Capabilities

Globalization 2.0 presents unprecedented challenges to governance – social networks, the emergence of megacities as large as entire nations, and the global division of tasks in the production process scattered across the planet owing to the mobility of skills, capital, and technology.

Social Networks

The arrival of social media in civil society is a game-changer for governance. For both America and China, the evolution of democracy must also mean figuring out how to balance the robust participatory power of social networks with the legitimate governing authority required to provide for the common good and the long term.

The power shift underway was well described by Mark Zuckerberg in his initial public offering letter to Facebook investors ahead of the company's stock market listing:

We hope to change how people relate to their governments and social institutions.

We believe building tools to help people share can bring a more honest and transparent dialogue around government that could lead to more direct empowerment of people, more accountability for officials and better solutions to some of the biggest problems of our time.

By giving people the power to share, we are starting to see people make their voices heard on a different scale from what has historically been possible. These voices will increase in number and volume. They cannot be ignored. Over time, we expect governments will become more responsive to issues and concerns raised directly by all their people rather than through intermediaries controlled by a select few.[1]

All that was solid about the established guilds, intermediaries, and custodians of perception is melting into air under the assault of "the age of amateurs"[2] unleashed by Zuckerberg and the other virtual Red Guards of Silicon Valley. Connectivity among the newly empowered voices is unraveling the last hanging threads of authority – cultural, social, and political – and weaving another pattern of power.

"Who, whom?" was the famous question Karl Marx asked as he set out in *Das Kapital*[3] to define the power relations of the highly stratified societies of early industrial capitalism. "Who controls whom?" is the question Twitter's Jack Dorsey asks about our societies, which are becoming ever more transparent as networks that distribute shared information equally undermine the control and authority of "gatekeepers" and empower the "gated."

As Dorsey has also noted, social media networks like Twitter or Facebook are utilities shaped by their users.

This reciprocal dependence, Karine Nahon[4] argues, creates a "fuzzy" balance of power between the utility and the user, the gatekeeper and the gated, that is ever-shifting. In the end, the gatekeepers in social networks maintain their power only through the "consent of the gated."

Similarly, governments which derive their legitimacy as "servants of the people" (China) or "democracies" (the West) can be considered utilities that are forced by the transparency of shared information to be responsive to the robust feedback enabled by social networks.

Nowhere is this power shift more evident than in China. The rise there of a vast and roiling "monitory webocracy" in recent years has changed the balance of power between citizens and the state-party. What *Transparent Society* author David Brin[5] calls "sous-veillance," or monitoring of the authorities from below, through *weibo*, on every issue from tainted milk and train wrecks to air pollution and official corruption, is doing in spades what Sun Yat-sen envisioned for his proposed "fifth branch" of government – the "Control *Yuan*," aimed at catching corrupt and incompetent officials.

The hierarchical meritocracy of China is an efficient system, but without feedback loops that provide reliable information, the meridians of the body politic become clogged and ultimately fail. In a sense, microblogs help solve this age-old problem of "insufficient feedback to the emperor," which has led to the fall of many an out-of-touch dynasty.

Eric X. Li and George Yeo have argued that this monitory webocracy has already become an organic part of the fabric of Chinese governance because the Communist Party uses it as an early warning feedback mechanism to correct policies that might undermine its performance-based legitimacy. By effectively processing criticism with acute responsiveness, the Party cements its hold on power.[6]

Who controls whom in such a circumstance? The gated or the gatekeeper?

Others are less starry eyed. John Keane,[7] who came up with the notion of "monitory democracy," reminds us of the multitude of censors lurking in all corners of cyberspace with Chinese characteristics searching for unauthorized keywords and regularly hauling in for "a cup of tea served with fear" those bloggers who persistently go too far.

No doubt both views of the situation in China are true and no one is sure where it will lead. It is a "giant petri dish" of possible outcomes.

The Italian Communist Party leader of the 1930s, Antonio Gramsci, argued that, without a Leninist party, the masses are an impotent "diaspora."[8] True to its Leninist bent, the Chinese Communist Party fully understands Gramsci's point from the perspective of power: no competition for the ruling narrative should be allowed even to sprout. For the CCP, the paradoxical role of a Leninist party in power is to make sure the masses *remain a diaspora*.

"Après nous, le Deluge" ("After us, the Deluge") is the conviction of China's more anxious hardliners looking out at the information age from behind the walled Forbidden City compound of Zhongnanhai where they live and work. They fear the loss of order and a slip back into the chaos of the Cultural Revolution. For them, Twitter and Facebook are "manufacturers of chaos." Nothing frightens them more than the idea of Red Guards on Twitter. In 2011, China's budget allocated more funds to "information security" than the military. They want to make sure that no two individuals who vent on the Net should ever be allowed to meet in the street.

What is not in doubt in China is that "the pendulum of power" is rapidly gaining momentum there. And that has major implications for the future if heavy instead of deft hands seize the lever of the state and try to impede the forces of gravity.

There are too many daily examples of China's netizen activists to inventory. The case of Wukan[9] in late 2011 and early 2012 is now the most famous. Citizens protesting a crooked land deal between local authorities and developers actually ran the authorities out of town and ruled themselves for weeks before reaching a negotiated settlement with the Party secretary of Guangdong province, Wang Yang, who in the end, as we noted in Chapter 2, appointed a leading protestor as the new village Party secretary. In that skirmish, netizens downloaded and shared satellite images of the contested land through Google Maps.

A citizen's protest that erupted in Nanjing in May 2011 is illustrative of the still uneven give and take that is common. Local citizens took to the microblogs and even protested in front of the city library against a city development plan that would tear down Nanjing's famous wutong trees to make way for new subway lines. Though citizens were not in the end able to alter the project in a significant way, the city authorities did establish a "Green Assessment Committee" with eight citizen members to review the plan, albeit outnumbered by nine "experts" from the government and construction companies.[10]

The participatory power of social media is no less consequential for open societies that will open further. "Monitory democracy" through the web is becoming the "fifth estate" as it supplants the role of the mainstream media as the "fourth estate" check of a free press on government.

In Japan, moms worried about how the Fukushima nuclear fallout might affect their children are connecting up on Mixi, a popular social networking website.[11]

The emergence of networked *Wutbürgers,* or "enraged citizens," has become a regular feature of political life in Germany. Neither right nor left, but nonpartisan, these groups linked through social media aim to defend their local interests, whether against the construction of nuclear power plants, rail lines, or airports in their communities.[12]

In June 2011, Italians, driven for the first time by a wide use of social media, turned out in droves in a referendum to reject plans for privatizing the water system and for the expansion of nuclear power plants. "I followed the run-up and projections on Twitter, and it changed my perspective," *The New York Times* quoted one voter as saying. "Politics in Italy is no longer just on TV."[13]

In late May 2011, a similar movement of *indignados* (the indignant) bloomed in Spain, occupying Madrid's Puerta del Sol as if it were Tahrir Square in Cairo.[14] Driven by social media, and neither left nor right, this mainly youthful movement protested the unresponsiveness of the mainstream party elites to their jobless woes.

Even in Saudi Arabia, the anonymous tweeter Mutjahadid has scandalized the nation with regular exposés of the corrupt dealings of the Royal Family, and women testing the rule against driving are connecting in support groups through Twitter.

Governments are getting the message and preparing for the challenge.

In his report to the 21st Century Council on the e-G-8 Summit hosted by then-President Sarkozy in

Paris in May 2011, Google's Eric Schmidt[15] noted that, if openness remains the norm, the Internet will make governments more accountable and enable more self-government. "Liberating government data," as he put it, has hugely positive benefits for the public. Further, "cloud computing" will enable a whole level of new government services because so many can share access to the same database.

As British Prime Minister David Cameron has written,

> Information is power. It lets people hold the powerful to account, giving them the tools they need to take on politicians and bureaucrats. It gives people new choices and chances, allowing them to make informed judgments about their future. And it lets our professionals judge themselves against one another, and our entrepreneurs develop new products and services.[16]

Cameron noted the popularity of the British government's new transparency program. When it published street-level crime maps in 2011 showing what crimes had been committed and exactly where, the government website had 18 million hits in one hour. The site also published evaluations of teachers and doctors in public schools and the health service.

Governance as usual may no longer be possible, but response and responsibility don't always coincide. "To answer to the needs of public opinion is necessary on the one hand," former Spanish premier Felipe González acknowledged, "but when we have political projects we must get over these immediate tensions that are created with the public, which is disorganized and responds to issues in a more spontaneous way." He also stated:

> They are not well organized as they once were with strong parties or unions, but they are nonetheless able to respond to the changing realities in a fragmented,

less cohesive way. So the political leadership must guide political changes but, by definition, the public in all its diverse manifestations will change its mind all the time. Now the big question is, how can we have political leadership with medium- or long-term goals with a more spontaneous, active and diverse public?[17]

Governance

Tempting though it may be to celebrate "amateurs like us" shaping the utility of powerful social networks, we should be no less wary than the American Founding Fathers of trading in monarchy for the mob unshackled from institutional restraints and unburdened by experience or expertise. The stodgy Framers contrived as children of the Enlightenment to put "the cool mind" of deliberative institutions (representative legislature, the non-elected Senate, the Supreme Court) between power and the direct exercise of popular will. Their aim was to avert tyranny of the populist majority as well as government by the inexperienced and unenlightened.

As we argue elsewhere and often in this book, one-person-one-vote electoral democracy is in crisis today because short-term self-interest expressed by the individual voter, unfiltered by strong deliberative institutions that have now eroded, does not collectively amount to what is in the long-term common interest for society. Retail rationality at the ballot box can easily add up to wholesale madness.

This can be seen most clearly in California, which practices the very kind of direct democracy through plebiscite that the Founding Fathers swore off after the sad experience of government under the Articles of Confederation, with the result that, to use once again this prime example, the state now absurdly spends more on prisons than on higher education.

82

The empowerment of amateurs and what we call the "Fox populi" over and against mediating elites and institutions through social networks is direct democracy on steroids. "Alerted to problems through shared information," David Brin says, "the two populisms of our present culture war in America – those against liberal culture and those against the 'smarty pants guild' of professional authority – act viscerally according to pre-set modules. Then you get a whole bunch of little Nuremberg rallies across the Internet."[18]

Without checks and balances, cyber-powered direct democracy can undermine instead of bolster good governance.

Some years ago, pondering the mediacracy that gave rise to Silvio Berlusconi, Gianni de Michelis, the Italian foreign minister at the time, argued that the West needed a "Montesquieu of the information age."[19] He noted:

> In their Constitution, the American founders understood that sound government must prevent rule by the pure wash of immediacy and populist emotion. If, for example, long-term common interests, such as preservation of the environment or human rights for all, are unable to check and balance the immediate interests of the consumer or the narrow fears of the racist, the unmediated reign of public opinion will end up destroying democracy itself.[20]

Smart Mobs

While the participatory power of social networks, as we have seen in Egypt and Tunisia, can tear down authority by mobilizing diasporas of the disaffected, we have yet to find through them the means for consensus-building that can establish the enduring legitimacy of governing authority required to provide for the common good and sustain society over the long term. You can't tweet a constitution.

As David Brin points out, "Twitter and Facebook are good for simple-minded coalescing of those resolved to act. But these interfaces collapse when it comes to the enlightenment processes of reasoned negotiations and problem solving."[21]

The crisis of governance today in democracies results from the "lack of deliberation." Deliberation is necessary so that democracy produces collectively intelligent decisions instead of dumb politics.

Without deliberative mechanisms for making decisions that weigh consequences and balance tradeoffs, social networks that only enhance unmediated participation and information also just enhance the "dumb mob."

Turning the "dumb mob" into the "smart mob" is one of the key challenges of good governance in the age of social media.

Bringing deliberative processes to cyberspace, augmenting the ability of *ad hoc* groups to gather information, analyze it, organize proposals and arguments, model outcomes, compare alternative approaches, and negotiate hybrid "positive sum" solutions –- all of these together might help forge the smart mob (millions of them) out of the dumb mobs that we've known until now.

As shown by deliberative polling experience – from California to China to Japan to Europe – the public is not as polarized as political elites. This is especially true in the US, where politicians are often driven to extremes because they have to appeal to the margins that mobilize in the primary process.

Consensus can emerge, however, when citizens – selected as indicative representatives of the electorate at

large through scientific sampling – are put in a depoliticized zone, or an "island of goodwill" beyond the reach
of the "persuasion industry" that dominates elections,
and given the facts and access to experts with contending points of view.

While deliberative polling has been done physically
– by bringing 200 or 500 people together through scientific sampling (not unlike in Athens 2,400 years ago,
where the assembly of 500 was chosen by lottery), it has
not been done virtually. The success of on-line seminars
by universities such as Stanford – where as many as
160,000 people participate virtually and then network
among each other – suggests the possibilities.

Editing and Governing

Neutral, objective, quality information is the basis for
solid deliberation.

Yet, here too, we face the same politicization and
polarization as in political life. Just as primaries drive
politics in democratic societies to polarized positions,
the imperative of "monetizing attention" for niche markets contaminates the objective quality of information,
which is edited to sell. Bloggers talk only to their own
tribe. People find only the information they are looking
for. Information becomes non-communication.

Curating information – sorting out intellectual quality
and truth claims or communicating across boundaries –
is akin to governance through deliberation.

Agile Meritocracy

Brin[22] further foresees a system based less on creden-
tials than on the earned credibility of "flowing, living,
breathing reputation." Since social networks and shared
knowledge continuously challenge elites and credentialed
meritocracy, it is likely the future will feature a new

"agile meritocracy" whose transient power rises and falls based on reputation and performance. This new meritocracy – a distant descendant of meritocratic testing, but far more self-organizing – might replace entrenched elites. More likely, it will add a vibrantly creative periphery, still requiring a core of highly responsive experts.

This idea of an "agile meritocracy" corresponds to what other network theorists have called "transient elites" thrown up by the ever-shifting "pendulum of power" that swings between the gated and the gatekeepers. As long as these elites are invested with the legitimacy of performance, they hold the allegiance of their users. If not, the users move on to look for other alternative utilities that give them what they want.

Without the kind of deliberative mechanism we've discussed, however, this acceleration of power transfer may well magnify the short-term, immediate gratification bias of consumer democracy. Tweets that bust trust with real-time information are also breaking bonds and boundaries that are difficult to re-establish. Deferred gratification and the long-term perspective will be even further eclipsed when the survival of transient elites depends on quick-fix policy responses or, in the case of the media, "monetizing attention" before the next fleeting click of the mouse.

A Common Narrative versus Disparate Connectivity
As we have also learned from the experiences of the "Facebook children" in Egypt and Tunisia, what matters most when it comes to sustained power is not connectivity, but a "common narrative" defined by and aligned with real social and economic interests. If users shape the utility of social media, it is the narrative that shapes the users. Networks may be intelligent, but they are not in and of themselves legitimate.

86

To be sure, performance must ultimately match the claims of the common narrative or authority and legitimacy will erode. But a shared narrative, not just shared information, is necessary to provide the patient allegiance required to allow policies for the long term to show fruition.

If at certain moments a kind of "flash narrative" crystallizes and can bring an otherwise disparate crowd of the connected into the streets, it cannot sustain them in the seats of power. For that, the hegemony of a shared worldview is necessary that ties people together into a unified mindset and defines with authority what is included and what is excluded from the political agenda. It is what the Islamic parties have in Egypt today. It is what the free spirits of Facebook lack.

Balancing Facebook and the Party

Good governance, then, requires a balance between the participatory power of social networks and governing authority established by a common narrative. The Beijing-blessed former chief executive of rambunctious Hong Kong, Tung Cheehwa,[23] has argued that social media are all well and good to express the concerns of the public, but "Facebook must be balanced by the Party." Of course, the opposite is true as well: the Party must be balanced by Facebook.

According to Norbert Wiener, "the father of cybernetics," humans respond to challenges in two ways: ontogenetically and phylogenetically. Ontogenetic activities are organized and carried out through centrally designed institutions to shape the development of society. The phylogenetic response is evolutionary, like self-organizing bacteria lacking foresight but responding to the environment.

This relationship, as George Yeo has posited, is both adversarial and symbiotic. Political authority today is ontogenetic and cyberspace is phylogenetic. Good governance and the health of human society depend on how these processes are balanced.

Sometimes it takes an institution. Crowd-sourced authority is good for some things, not others. It is good for innovation and protest; it is bad for governance.

It is a libertarian illusion to believe that distributed networks of amateurs or "unknown experts" can self-administer a society based on rational self-interested decisions. It was, after all, the distributed networks of financial experts that instigated the Wall Street meltdown. It was up to the stodgy old "drunk uncle" institution of the US government to salvage the system.

What we are suggesting here, as throughout this book, is a new "hybrid" model of governance that accommodates the complexity of more diverse players through hierarchical structures with authority and capacity, more consensus-building processes, and, at the same time, more feedback loops to ensure reciprocal accountability.

There is not one answer. A given balance within the operating system of governance will work or not work depending on the conditions. Success will only result from the "field effect" of bringing all the right elements to bear as the circumstances on the ground demand. One-person-one-vote, just like meritocratic rule, must be scaled to the circumstances.

The same happens within companies as well. Google required one kind of governance, more reciprocal and collegial, when it was only 500 innovating employees. With 50,000 employees and globe-spanning markets, complexity requires more hierarchy for efficiency's sake. Yet innovation must retain its own space or efficiency will kill it off.

In short, governance is an open-ended operating system based on what works. The most adaptable will survive.

Megacities: The Past Is Too Small to Inhabit

It is not surprising that the intellectual trajectory of the Spanish scholar Manuel Castells has taken him from urbanology[24] to communications and network theory.[25]

For Castells, the megacities that have emerged in the 21st century – as large as whole nations with populations of between 10 and 20 million – are becoming less a "space of places" than a "space of flows" where the in-migrating masses meet electronic networks that connect distant nodes of information, business, decision-making, and advanced services. Instead of generators of distinct culture, megacities are becoming sprawling "zones of highly mobile people and information."[26]

According to the McKinsey Global Institute, most cities of this size will arise in Asia over the next 15 years.[27] Already Tokyo, Seoul, Shanghai, and Mumbai have populations near 20 million, as do São Paulo and Mexico City in Latin America.

As their historical identity of place is weakened, these urban zones are increasingly linked as "one global city," tied together virtually by the planetary reach of the media and economically through trade, finance, and the global scattering of productive capability. This creates a new dichotomy: the more powerful cities like London and Mumbai or regions like Silicon Valley become in their global role, the more they are divorced from their territorial hinterland.

The Dutch architect and urban theorist Rem Koolhaas[28] has similarly argued that the concentration of population in megacities increasingly shaped more by the global forces of trade, production, consumption, and finance than by local historical identity has made "the past too small to inhabit," giving birth to the kind of "generic city" one sees all across Asia, particularly in China. To Koolhaas, the "new norm has been synthesized in Singapore – a hard core Confucian shamelessness, a kind of ultimate power of efficiency that will fuel the modernization of Asia."[29]

Yet, the very complexity of the wired, globalized megacity, and the inevitable new sprouts of diversity that human nature forces up through cracks in the slabs of conformity, challenge the best intensions of authoritarian hierarchy. Even in the megacity designed for efficiency, the metropolitan condition reemerges where, as Koolhaas says, many events take place simultaneously and spontaneously without coordination, "like the Internet."[30]

Singapore's George Yeo[31] understands this, having lost his parliamentary constituency for Lee Kuan Yew's ruling People's Action Party in 2011 in a campaign where social media challenged the city-state's distant, insular paternalistic elite.

For Yeo, the Internet expresses the complexity of urban relationships today which profoundly unsettle the traditional hierarchies of the rural-agricultural order upon which Confucianism was founded. The same is true of China's Communist Party. Organized as a peasant movement, it now rules a country where half the population is urban.

As we have argued throughout this book, if China's modern mandarinate doesn't create participatory space for that vast country's increasingly connected urban voices – as Singapore is being forced to do through its quasi-open political space – its brittle authority will break. Conversely, as we have also argued, if technologically empowered diversity further erodes any sense of civic commonality in the West, democracy, divided against itself, will fail. Facing a common future, each needs to find balance in its own way.

Self-Governing Feedback

Finding that balance entails resolving a paradox. The intensification of participatory feedback loops through close urban connectivity can enable self-governance to become more intelligent. As the architect and ecologist Paolo Soleri[32] has posited, the distance and time that block information response will be virtually obliterated by wired density, thus mimicking the miniature circuitry of the brain.

For Twitter's Jack Dorsey, the "time to recognition"[33] through tight feedback loops of instant connection can aid the quality of governance because it enables the effective use of the best information in real time.

Yet, by amplifying individual behavior several millionfold, the collective impact of personal choice in the mega-urban condition can also harm the common good. After a certain threshold, as we see everywhere today from Istanbul to Beijing, the individual mobility of countless automobiles can add up to the immobility of congested gridlock. The carbon exhaust of millions of individual cars in cities with millions of people can add up to climate change.

To realize its potential, the mega-urban world needs a new "civic software" that not only fosters the intelligence of connectivity through transparency and participation but also balances empowered individuals and social networks with institutions that filter short-term, self-interested choices.

In environmental terms, the efficient intelligence of wired density will necessarily clash with the industrialized desire of consumer culture driven by personal choice. Frugality, the wise husbanding of scarce resources, will become the premier civic virtue of an urban planet.

Here, too, the new "civic software" that balances individual and community consists of devolving, involving, and decision-division.

It doesn't trade in newness for nostalgia of the no longer habitable past, but reasserts the political and cultural identity of place against the "space of flows" to create an equilibrium between local identity and global interdependence. It seeks to leverage networks, instead of being leveraged by them, through strengthening the nodes of governance where proximity between ruler and ruled makes it most legitimate. Cities are also the largest scale at which individuals and small *ad hoc* groups can still make a big difference. They are the global locus where problems that are both too large and too small for the nation-state must be resolved.

Particularly on global issues like climate change where it is hard to reach agreements by global summitry, city-regions or subnational polities like the American states or the Chinese provinces – after all, the chief generators of carbon gases that warm the atmosphere – can take more effective and direct action than can nation-states. For example, cities like Portland, Hangzhou, and New York, like the state of California, have taken their own action and joined with others at the subnational level to implement clean growth strategies.

Though linked together through globalization, city-regions or city-states can adopt different social values from others, or join others beyond their national borders who share those values. As Daniel Bell and Avner de-Shalit have pointed out:

> The idea that cities have a distinctive ethos – a shared way of life that informs the thinking and judgments of its inhabitants – has a long history. In the ancient world, Athens was synonymous with democracy and Sparta represented military discipline. Jerusalem expressed religious values, and the twin cities that made up the Zhou dynasty's capital at Louyang flourished as a commercial metropolis.[34]

Putting a rather more positive spin than Rem Koolhaas on the significance of Singapore's experience, George Yeo sees the future in megacity regions where the past may have become too small to inhabit but the nation-state, and certainly the integrated world, is too large to govern. "The information revolution," he says, "will not dissolve the world into an amorphous mass of weakened political entities, but transform it into more efficient units of power – crossroads cities like the big city-states in Europe and China before the age of empire."[35]

Looking at city-states as distinctive nodes in a global network is also key to the strengthening the legitimacy of governance in an interdependent world of plural identities. The co-existence of plural jurisdictions linked by common interests but not reduced to a common identity is the commodious *modus vivendi* by which the local/global conundrum can be resolved. "One world, but many systems" that achieves autonomy through devolution is the alternative both to the "clash of civilizations" and to the "end of history" in which one global model fits all.

In a similar vein to George Yeo's vision, the British philosopher John Gray has also speculated that the circumstance we are moving into is "more like the late Middle Ages" than the early modern period. Gray writes:

> The Middle Ages were a time of plural jurisdictions, a time before the Treaty of Westphalia when the absolutist claims of the modern state hadn't yet been accepted. I tend to share Isaiah Berlin's judgment that, in some respects, the Middle Ages were more civilized and more peaceable than our time of world wars. And that is precisely because all those plural jurisdictions had to negotiate with each other over their powers and interests, none powerful enough to simply dominate the other.[36]

Though for now the nation-state still remains the mainframe of identity, the advent of networks, the reach of the media, globe-spanning supply chains, and the specialized division of labor in global production, as we will discuss in the next section, all contribute to the emergent possibility of crossroad city-regions becoming the key locus of governance in a globalized world.

Globally Scattered Productive Capabilities

The power of cities and their immediate regions has grown to such an extent on this urban planet that mayors can wield as much clout as national leaders. Only 600 cities produce 60 percent of global GDP.[37] These "delocalized" nodes of connectivity and population concentration increasingly delinked from their hinterlands have also become the key entrepôts of mobile skills, capital, and technology in the global division of production capabilities. The fragmentation of the manufacturing process, enabled by an array of technological advances, from container vessels to real-time logistics, is altering the traditional patterns of trade and employment based on the nation-state framework. Today, products are not so much made in China or the US or Europe, but "made in the world" through supply chains strung out across a global archipelago of production sites.

As Singapore has shown, city-states are more efficient and nimble political units than cumbersome, slow-moving nations in adjusting quickly to the ever-shifting global mobility of capital, technology, and tasks. The local tax and regulatory environment as well as educational systems can be more flexible to attract the migration of industry, services, and skills that create wealth.

There is no better expert on how globally scattered production impacts trade and employment than Pascal Lamy, the director general of the World Trade Organization:

> Fully 60 percent of Asian countries' international trade is concentrated in the Asian zone itself, the area which has witnessed the most in-depth integration of its production chains, with the manufacture of parts and semi-assembled units that are then mixed with components which themselves comprise elements from different countries, and the whole then ends up in China for assembly before being exported to the US, Europe and elsewhere.
>
> The process of fragmentation among different countries and types of labor is effectively illustrated by the production chain of certain emblematic products such as the iPad, a part of which is assembled in Chengdu, in western China.
>
> Over 100,000 people work in a factory that only "manufactures" one part, namely the iPad's aluminum casing. The rest of the factory's activity consists of alternating assembly operations with technical testing.
>
> Logistics circuits are enormously complex, and it

takes eight hours to assemble the components of an iPad on account of the large number of quality controls required. The Chinese added value generated by this factory accounts for 5 percent of the iPad's purchase price, while the American added value of the same iPad, assembled in China and exported to the United States, is over 20 times higher.

Global manufacturing chains are constantly changing, in an ongoing movement involving the allocation and reallocation of labor and capital in response to the opportunities that businesses perceive, to a changing regulatory environment, and to changes in trade barriers. The execution of these tasks, once performed in a given country by a given company and based on the use of an extensive labor force, can now be brutally shifted to another country and another company with different means of production.

It is no longer a matter of trading in goods and services but of "trading in tasks."[38]

How the costs and benefits of globalization can be spread more evenly across the emergent city-regions and their emptying hinterlands as a result of this process Lamy describes is one of the greatest challenges to governance under Globalization 2.0.

While this capacity to go globally wherever production can be most efficient spreads growth and employment around the planet, especially in the emerging economies, it also shifts opportunities away from the older, more expensive labor markets in the advanced world.

This obviously spells bad news for countries in Europe with extensive social welfare systems, or even the US with its generously pledged pensions once paid for with middle-class manufacturing jobs. As Lamy worries, "[S]ocial and economic fabrics cannot develop at the same pace."[39] Because of global competition, people in the advanced economies are forced to work harder and longer for less pay. Income distribution worsens and politics in those countries with prominent losers make it harder to forge a common global response to this huge structural shift.

The best option for the advanced countries as their share of manufacturing drops well below the 30 percent of world product it maintained in the post-World War II period is not to seek "price competitiveness" through a race to the bottom. Rather, it is to seek to attract the "non-price competitive" tasks of production, such as innovation, high skills, and value-added services. This depends on cutting-edge information and physical infra- structure, excellence in education and training, as well as a conducive quality of life in the city-regions that host the global economy.

The city-regions and nation-states of the advanced world need a strategic agenda to address this structural challenge instead of drifting along and hoping for the best.

At the Paris meeting of the 21st Century Council in October 2011, both Michael Spence and Mohammed El-Erian[40] rightly argued that the way for the advanced economies to get back on track is to jettison the "cyclical mentality" that assumes they will bounce back after recession and adopt instead the "structural mentality" aimed at building up investments in edu- cation and infrastructure that will improve non-price competitiveness.

In order for nations or city-regions to adapt to this new global division of labor, trade balances must be cal- culated anew in a way that reflects where value is added to the end product instead of from whence a product is exported or to where it is imported.

As Lamy puts it,

[B]ilateral trade imbalances are becoming meaningless when China's exports to the United States contain almost 50 percent of Chinese added value while U.S. exports to China contain 80 percent to 90 percent of American added value. It is economic nonsense to continue to calculate bilateral trade balances the way we do today. What we need to monitor is the effective added value in each country, not the overall value of goods and services imported and exported.[41]

This new reality of trade flows owing to globally scattered production and the emergence of ever-more autonomous city-regions below the level of the nation-state – but linked globally – suggests the potential for a 21st-century equivalent of the prosperous Hanseatic League along the Baltic from the 13th to the 17th century.

What LinkedIn founder Reid Hoffman discovered in the professional landscape of Silicon Valley will apply as well to the new trading and producing web of city-regions: "Identities are established by who you connect with and how you put together your network. Networks will increase stability and productivity. When you drive economic decisions through a network you have a much more intelligent and adaptive system."[42]

A NOTE ON THE DISTRIBUTION OF WEALTH

The creative opportunities presented by the knowledge economy, competitive megacities, mobile factors of production, productivity-enhancing network technologies, and the global scale of markets are immense. But they also entail destructive de-linkages of a scope that might make Karl Marx relevant again.

The divorce of cities and regions – with their concentrations of mega-billionaire individuals and companies with access to global markets – from the hinterland of the rest of their country is one such de-linkage. This conjoins with the increasing divorce of productivity and wealth based on technology and global networks from employment. Thus the new reality of rich countries with poor people and poor countries with rich people – a planet of slums beneath the glitter of globalization like Ambani's high-rise palace in Mumbai, or a $100 billion market valuation for Facebook, but an 11 percent unemployment rate in its home state, California.

It is this combination of global scale, productivity leaps, and the concentration of wealth separated from territory and population that resurrects the specter of Marx. If good governance can't deliver inclusive growth, it will have to deliver redistribution in some form or another.

Notably, some Chinese economists regard a mixed economic system – a combination of large state enterprises along with private enterprise – as key to being able to bridge the gap into which so many fall during the creative-destructive process of innovation. Slowing innovation to ensure stable employment is seen as socially efficient even if it hinders market efficiency.

ROOTLESS POWER

As the futurist Alvin Toffler pointed out decades ago in his book *The Third Wave*,[43] knowledge has supplanted both land and smokestack industries as the primary basis of wealth in our time. The speed with which the information technologies have entered our lives and amplified our capacities has surpassed the established means, such as the gross domestic product, of measuring their impact. Traditional measurements fail to capture the vastly increased – indeed game-changing – value of technology.

The value added by a ready Google search, a LinkedIn connection, a Facebook friend, or leapfrog cellular communication where no landlines exists is incalculable through measures of physical units of production. What are today information companies worth billions were started in dorm rooms with no capital other than the algorithmic imagination in the minds of geeks.

In such a world, power is access to knowledge. Because the entry threshold is theoretically available to anyone with a mind and a mobile device, it also means that the skills associated with the power of knowledge can be anywhere or go anywhere. Whoever possesses such mobile capacity is not bound – functionally or morally – to nation, tribe, hinterland, or community. This creates not only opportunity, but also inequality.

Each system of governance must adapt in its own way to the participatory power of social networks, the emergence of megacities, and the global division of labor that scatters the tasks of production across the planet, or fail. In each case the solution lies in the three principles of intelligent governance – devolve, involve, and decision-division.

In the following chapter, we develop the template of intelligent governance in detail.

Part II

Intelligent Governance

Theory and Practice

5

Intelligent Governance*

Tenets and Template

Introduction

As we have discussed, the new conditions of global interdependence and growing diversity amplified by the new technologies of the knowledge society both require and enable more intelligent structures of governance, from the level of the emergent megacities – some as large as whole nations – to the nation-state, which, despite its weakening ramparts, still remains the main source of historical identity.

While any system of governance, as we have also observed, can remain legitimate only through accommodating the new reality of distributed power through new forms of participation, it must at the same time find effective means to manage complexity at the highest levels, both within states and nations and among them.

---

* The ideas that appear on the following pages in this "exercise in political imagination" emerged through a series of discussions over many months in 2010 between the authors and a small group of scholars that included Bin Wong, Director of the Asia Institute at UCLA; Tom Schwarz, professor of political science, UCLA; and Marty Kaplan, director of the Norman Lear Center and research professor at the Annenberg School of Communication at the University of Southern California.

Knowledgeable Democracy

In practice this means that decision-making power must be decentralized as much as possible to communities of active citizens in the domains of their competence. In short, it must *devolve* and *involve* beyond the old systems of a mass public choosing distant rulers in periodic one-person-one-vote elections where their voice doesn't matter. An "intelligent electorate" is part and parcel of a *knowledgeable democracy.*

Accountable Meritocracy

To manage the interdependence, interactions, and integration of such widely distributed power, greater political capacity must also be established at the top to take the long view of the system as a whole – *decision-division* based on capability. Those who inhabit these heights must possess not only the requisite technical expertise, but also the practical wisdom of experience and knowledge of historical precedent. They must, in effect, be a learned meritocracy.

Unlike Plato's guardians or China's ancient scholar-rulers, however, a meritocratic class in the knowledge age cannot be a power unto itself and must necessarily be held accountable.

While intentionally insulated from the immediate, special-interest pressures of electoral democracy, legitimacy dictates that any meritocratic body must nonetheless be regularly aerated so it doesn't become hidebound. It must be institutionally checked by the publics and democratically elected representatives that delegate authority to it. In today's "transparent society," widely shared information among the networked public – "monitory democracy" – will necessarily provide an additional check on the meritocracy the way it does on any professional capacity.

The main challenge of designing a sustainable system of good governance is guarding against special-interest influence and a politics dominated by short-term populist pressures, magnified by the real-time direct democracy of social media, while at the same time engaging the broadest public participation to ensure accountability and consent.*

In this chapter, we propose a template that seeks to achieve "intelligent governance" by combining the responsible democracy of a knowledgeable electorate *organized on a human scale* with accountable meritocracy.

The Good Society

A good society cannot determine outcomes, but it can give everyone an equal start in life, allowing for achievement by the exceptional and entrepreneurial without thwarting the chances of the less ambitious. Clearly, market-driven economies are the best generators of job opportunities and wealth. Competition also forces more disciplined government.

Under the ideal social compact of intelligent governance, government would provide the means of well-being and personal self-realization for all through social minimums, the guarantee of basic human rights, free expression, and the effective rule of law.† Needless

---

* This is one of Francis Fukuyama's main lessons after his exhaustive examination of the history of the rise and decay of the best state practices in the Ottoman Empire and the long millennia of the Chinese mandarinate (F. Fukuyama, *The Origins of Political Order: From Prehuman Times to the French Revolution*, New York: Macmillan, 2011).

† Under "intelligent governance," a Bill of Rights protecting individual freedoms would be a part of the constitution: freedom of conscience/religion (i.e. secular state); freedom of expression; freedom of association/forms of family life; the right to privacy; and moral freedom for all if its exercise entails no harm to others.

to say, the utopian objective of a social minimum is no less desirable, even though it is far from economic and political reality in most places on the planet. Yet, imagining what constitutes a just and good society, as everyone from Karl Marx[1] to John Rawls[2] has argued, is bound to start with this idea. To be sure, the challenges of designing an economic system with the right set of incentives and penalties that will make it both fair and efficient are great indeed. The ideal itself remains a measure of moral ambition that should guide intelligent governance.

In any balanced society, rights must be married to obligations. In return for guaranteed social minimums and other "public goods," individuals would be expected to participate responsibly as informed and civically literate citizens of their community. A networked,

---

Justice will be swift and transparent under the rule of law, including habeas corpus.

Guaranteed social minimums of the social compact of intelligent governance will include: universal healthcare; affordable housing and food security; quality education; the right to employment and choice of occupation and its location; access to communications and technology; a clean, healthy environment; access to government administration and services; and the provision of personal security and government pursuit and upholding of peace with other nations.

In addition, citizens can claim the positive rights to leisure, cultural opportunities to create and cultivate, convivial community, and diversity of lifestyles.

Singapore, for example, provides these minimums with a keen understanding of human nature and the art of governance. While the city-state maintains a hardline against corruption, it guarantees transportation opportunities, quality education, and decent housing, cementing its people to the system and building in its legitimacy. While targeting the poor who fall behind with subsidies for housing and minimum income, Singapore's leaders have been careful to root out any sense of entitlement that might lead to a culture of welfare dependence. For example, their Workfare program requires working for benefits from a charity fund dispensed by the prime minister. In other words, there are no guarantees without the responsibility of working in return.

flexi-time society allows much greater investment of time and commitment by the citizen in affairs beyond their own private lives.

Just as it proposes a better balance between the rights and duties of citizens, intelligent governance proposes to counterbalance populist and partisan impulses by institutionalizing the perspective of the long term and common good in a strong deliberative body insulated from direct electoral politics as well as establishing a capable, independent administration beyond the reach of special interests.

The power of citizens to influence "intelligent governance" should be relative to the extent of their alert and informed participation in the political life of the community. Citizens who choose to disengage as active participants can do so in the expectation that their consent to the delegation of authority obliges quality and competence in administration. The less power the citizenry choose to take on, the more they implicitly grant to governing institutions.

Intelligent governance is anti-bureaucratic. Government should be smart, but also as lean as possible – strong but limited. The issue is not big or small government, but good governance in which power is decentralized and distributed where appropriate and authority is delegated where competence dictates.

Template of Intelligent Governance

The best way to ensure intelligent governance would be through a mixed constitutional democracy that combines active participation of citizens at the community level and democratic elections for a legislature and chief executive who in turn delegate authority through

selective appointment to independent meritocratic institutions. As a final check on power, the electorate at
large would be empowered through periodic referenda
to evaluate government policies.

Such a constitutional democracy would be divided
into several independent branches. Those branches are:
(a) legislative, with an indirectly elected lower house
and selected upper house; (b) an executive elected by
the lower house; (c) and a selected Quadrumvirate
collective presidency. Independent authority would be
delegated to (d) the judiciary, (e) the central bank, (f)
the Human Resources Agency, and (g) the Government
Integrity Office. The general electorate, as noted above,
would have the ultimate recourse of periodic referenda
policies.

Constitutionally guaranteed free expression is of
fundamental importance in order to enable a robust
"monitory democracy" by civil society outside the
formal structures of government, including through
social networks and media. Because of the vast proliferation of media platforms and the consequent
hyper-barrage of information in the 21st century, an
independent media agency that is the benchmark for
objective, neutral information – albeit with the necessary safeguards against political control – would need
to be established as the requisite foundation for democratic deliberation.

Undoubtedly, the moral and political issues associated with technologies that change the boundaries of
the human condition would call, one day, for societal
oversight – perhaps even an agency like the World Health
Organization that assures access as well as protects the
public in areas from stem cell research to nuclear power.

The key features of intelligent governance are illus-
trated in Figure 5.1.

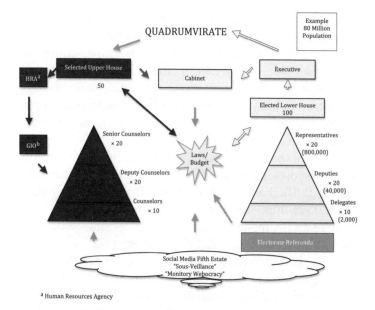

Figure 5.1 Features of intelligent governance
(courtesy of Alexander Gardels)

Community-Based Democracy

All citizens could participate through universal suffrage
in a one-person-one-vote stepped system of elections. In
our example of a four-level pyramidal structure starting at a broad base, human-scale associations of citizens would elect qualified delegates who in turn would
elect qualified deputies. Those deputies would then
elect qualified representatives who elect members of a
parliament/legislature.

In a complementary manner meant to encourage close
collaboration between government administrators and
citizens, administrative officials would be assigned to
deliver public services and monitor performance at each
parallel level of election.

The aim of a pyramidal structure of governance is to foster human-scale community-building – horizontal power – through active grass-roots associations of knowledgeable and well-informed voters. Local votes for faraway offices undermine the legitimacy of large democracies because they diminish the meaningful input of the individual voter. It is a form of disenfranchisement disguised as participation.

In our example, a country of 80 million inhabitants would be divided into 100 large districts (constituencies of 800,000). Each of those districts would be divided into 20 medium-size districts (40,000 constituents), and each of those medium-sized districts would be divided into 20 small districts (2,000 constituents).

Every small district would elect ten local delegates, each representing 200 voters. By using STV, or single transferable voting, in districts, the elected delegates would reflect a microcosm of the electorate as a whole. (This system is used in Australia, Ireland, and Cambridge, Massachusetts, among other places. Essentially, in successive rounds of voting, preferences are transferred to the remaining candidates after each round of elimination until a winning quota is reached. The system provides incentives for inter-party accommodation through this reciprocal exchange of preferences. STV also provides a better chance of electing popular independent candidates than those on a party list because voters are choosing between candidates, not parties.)

Those ten delegates would meet, deliberate, and elect one of their members as the deputy to a 20-member regional council, which in turn elects one of its members as a representative to a 20-member provincial council. Each provincial council then elects one member to the parliament/legislature, totaling 100 members in all. This means the parliament member/legislator would be directly beholden to 20 electors with whom effective communication and deliberation could take place (as opposed to the 800,000/1 ratio if he or she was directly elected by the public at large).

Each higher level of representation is not just a matter of election by the lower levels. Candidates would have to demonstrate capabilities – knowledge and experience – commensurate with the higher level of responsibility.

The reason for this indirect approach to electing a parliament/legislature through a pyramid structure is to remove the distance between the representative and represented at each level. The larger the constituency, the greater distance there will be between the individual citizen and the person he or she elects. Yet, the smaller the constituency, the more unwieldy the legislative body because it will have so many members that considered deliberation cannot take place. The solution is to break down the political system into workable, human-scale units, with each body successively electing the next.

In this successively elected, base-to-top pyramidal structure, electors at each level would thus have a more effective voice in setting the political agenda through an emphasis on small group deliberation; they would also have greater responsiveness from government through coordination with administrative counselors assigned to their respective level to implement policies and provide services. Close collaboration and feedback – including through the intensive use of social media – would constitute a grassroots public check on the bureaucracy.

What might be lost through directly electing a member of parliament by the electorate at large would be more than gained through citizens achieving a real voice in their affairs through quality of deliberation and proximity to their elected official at their level of participation.

All citizens would be eligible to vote, but should be

given every incentive and provided with every means to be responsibly informed.

Candidates would have to obtain a minimum number of signatures and have demonstrated community leadership and experience or obtained a minimum-level score on a comprehensive civics/issues test to stand for election. All candidates would have to state their positions on a full list of public issues at hand so they would not only be judged for single-issue stances, but display their full knowledge, or lack thereof, on all important issues of the day. Since all would have to express their positions on all relevant issues, the voters would have a clear idea of what they can expect from the leaders they elect, creating a level playing field of candidates.

A Fair Political Practices Commission of independent citizens would monitor all elections to make sure there are no irregularities and to call out false claims in the media. A joint committee of citizens and experts at each level would draw up the issues list to which candidates must respond.

THE QUALITY OF VOTERS

Democracy works best when voter capacity is of a high quality. Some have argued that voters should be rated so their vote can be weighted. In such a scenario, testing that might range from knowledge of the law to relevant issues in a given election would result in a score, say, of 1–5. The higher the voter capacity, as registered by his or her score, the more his/her vote would count.

Chad Hurley, the inventor of YouTube, is among those who have suggested voter weighting according to voters' knowledge of the affairs on which they are casting their ballot. Paradoxically, he argues, since the knowledge society is more complex, it is critical that voters possess a certain prerequisite of knowledge so that democracies inundated by information don't end up ruling out of ignorance or misinformation.[3]

In his 2006 book *The Myth of the Rational Voter*, Bryan Caplan, who also calls for weighted voter tests, cites the economist Frederic Bastiat, saying that

> the right to suffrage rests on the presumption of capacity. . . . And why is capacity a cause for exclusion? Because it is not the voter alone who must bear the consequences of his vote; because each vote involves and affects the whole community; because the community has the right to require some guarantee as to the acts on which its welfare and existence depend.[4]

Given the history of discrimination (i.e. property ownership, race) that has accompanied tests of voter capacity in the past, however, it is hard to imagine any extant democracy adopting such a practice today.

Nonetheless, it is clear that responsible choices by an informed electorate are the best defense of democracy. An uninformed electorate making consequential decisions only harms democracy.

A more viable option, which we discuss in more detail in the following chapter, might be the kind of "deliberative polling" on major issues in which delegates selected from among the general public (by scientific sampling) study and debate key questions over a period of time and then issue their recommendations to the rest of the public before a vote.

This method of "indicative representation" of the public at large through scientific sampling is a more refined version of the Athenian *polis*, where the Council of 500 was chosen by lottery.

Two Houses of Parliament

The parliament/legislature will have two houses.

The **lower house** would be elected through the stepped system just described; the **upper house** would be appointed in part by the executive and the lower house along with the "Quadrumvirate," or collective presidency, which itself would be appointed by the executive and approved by the lower house. In part, the upper house would also be composed of eligible citizens selected by random scientific sampling as indicative representatives of the public at large.

The main responsibilities of the lower house would be to elect the chief executive, approve appointments to the upper house, initiate and promulgate legislation, and approve budgets. The lower house members would be elected for five-year terms. No term limits would be imposed. No active outside business activities would be allowed. No other government positions could be held simultaneously.

Members of the lower house would be checked and balanced by the non-elected upper house chosen by meritocratic criteria mixed with indicative citizen representatives. Both houses would have to vote to pass legislation and approve the budget. A majority vote of at least 51 percent in each house would be required. However, if there was 60 percent support in the upper house, only 40 percent would be required in the lower house to pass legislation (and vice versa). This would avoid political gridlock that exists when partisan minorities can block legislation or debate.

A supermajority of the lower house would be required to overturn an executive veto.

To remove a government, a vote of "constructive no confidence" would be required – that is, a new coalition capable of replacing the one being routed would have to be in the position to take over governance.

The lower house must approve the nominees put forward for the Quadrumvirate, or collective presidency, by the chief executive.

Deliberation is as much at the heart of good governance as representation. In order to insulate the deliberative process from short-term political and constituent pressures, and thus enhance the long-term perspective, the upper house would be non-elected.

In our example, 20 members of this body of 50 distinguished and experienced leaders from the arts, academia, science, business, and previous government posts would be appointed by the Quadrumvirate. Twenty of the appointments would be apportioned to the executive and the lower house leadership. Ten of the members would be chosen by random scientific sampling as indicative representatives of the public at large. The point is to "aerate" the inside perspective of experts with the concerns of the average citizen. Upper house members would serve eight-year terms.

Selection of the upper house would be based on the general merit of experience and expertise, not on the basis of constituency representation. Because they would be in part selected by elected officials as well as the Quadrumvirate, there would be a measure of accountability to the democratic electorate as a whole – but only indirectly so as to limit political considerations. Because they would be randomly chosen, citizen members would also be insulated from political influence. In effect, the upper house would straddle the divide between meritocratic expertise and democratic accountability.

The main responsibilities of the upper house would be to act as public trustees bearing the long-term and bigger picture in mind, not the particular interests of constituents, as well as to oversee the non-political administrative branches of government. The upper house could propose legislation, provide the "second reading" function with the lower house, and negotiate legislative compromises. It would also be empowered to review and recommend the "sunsetting" of laws (i.e. laws would be set to remain in place for a limited number of years and would be reviewed if they were to continue).

The upper house would appoint the heads of the Human Resources Agency and the Government Integrity Office. It would have to approve the executive's nominations for the central bank and the Supreme Court.

Compensation would be competitive with comparable levels of competence and capacity in the private sector. All active business interests, as well as formal political affiliation, would be given up by sitting members.

On a regular basis over their eight-year term, the performance of members would be rated by the Human Resources Agency.

The Executive

In our example, the government leader, or executive, would be elected by a majority vote of the lower house. He/she would be tasked, as in an ideal "Westminster system," with formulating and presenting the budget for an "up or down vote" approval by both houses and have the power of veto. He/she would nominate the members of the collective presidency, or Quadrumvirate, who would have to be approved by the lower house. He/she would also nominate, for lower house approval, 20 members of the upper house.

A five-year term in office would be consistent with that of the lower house.

A veto could be overridden by a combined supermajority vote of both houses. The government leader could be removed by a supermajority vote of either the upper or lower house.

He/she would appoint a cabinet chief for each ministry approved by the upper house.

The government leader and cabinet ministers would receive compensation equivalent to private sector posts. No active business interests would be allowed.

An alternative to this parliamentary version of choosing an executive would be direct election by the entire electorate in order to produce a stronger executive, as in a presidential system. To avoid such an election becoming a mere "popularity contest," the legislature would chose five candidates from among its members as a pool of nominees from which the public can choose. The elected leader from among those five would thus possess the double mandate of having been chosen by their peers and the public at large.

In this alternative, budgets proposed by the directly elected executive would have to be negotiated with the legislative branch rather than presented for an up or down vote as in the Westminster parliamentary system.

Moral Power above the Fray

The **Quadrumvirate,** or collective presidency of four members, is a council of distinguished elder statespersons who would represent the unity of the society and the long-term perspective and continuity of the culture. Its members would be nominated by the executive of the government and approved by the lower house.

Moral influence would be their main tool and stewardship of the society as a whole their main charge. Their responsibility would be to select 20 of the members of the upper house and to schedule regular referenda by the public on key policies of the government.

This body would act as a kind of "council of elders" standing above the operational fray of politics and governance. Their role would be to provide symbolism of the whole and a sense of unity and harmony, especially in ethnically, religiously, and culturally diverse societies.

Terms would be seven years, so they would be out of sync with the electoral cycle, thus reducing political influence and sustaining independence of judgment.

Excellence, Honesty, and Transparency in Administration

A highly trained civil service, compensated on competitive terms with the private sector, would have to pass examinations to qualify for a position. No active business interests would be allowed. Personnel would have to be nonpartisan.

An independent **Human Resources Agency (HRA)** would recruit, examine, place, rotate, and monitor the performance of the civil service personnel. It would also pair administrative counselors with the stepped constituencies of the electoral pyramid. The aim would be to foster a competitive, goal-focused environment in the bureaucracy while ensuring responsiveness to the public. The top officials of the HRA would be nominated by the upper house and approved by the lower house.

He/she could be removed by a supermajority of either house. HRA personnel would have to be nonpartisan and have no active business interests.

To maintain excellence and internal competitiveness, the HRA would rate administrators (entry, interim, and exit), rotate them geographically (to avoid local cronyism) and across civil service functions based on performance competition, and promote and demote them so that the best man/woman fits a given post. Citizens would also be polled regularly to rate administrators with whom they interact, and the results would be published or posted on-line.

Proven good administrators would be elevated to ever more responsible positions, taking lessons from policies that worked in one area and transplanting them where possible elsewhere. In this way, meritocratic excellence would be emphasized over local political connections and private interests. A maximum term of service of ten years in any position would be enforced to prevent entrenchment with local interests and cronyism.

An Independent **Government Integrity Office (GIO)**, appointed by the head of the HRA and approved by the upper house, would oversee performance and rectitude of both elected and non-elected legislators, the executive and the administrative institutions. To encourage an active and engaged "monitory democracy" of citizens on the web, all non-security related government activities and transactions would be made transparently available through cloud computing under the auspices of the Office.

Members could be removed by a supermajority vote of either house. GIO members and staff would have to be nonpartisan and have no active business interests.

The GIO would have subpoena power in order to command evidence and testimony and could recommend prosecution to law enforcement authorities. The GIO would partner with the netizens of relevant communities to encourage "monitory webocracy" and set up procedures for rapid response.

Public Recourse

Periodic referenda would be regularly scheduled by the Quadrumvirate to enable the electorate as a whole to voice their approval or dissent over key policies of the government. Voting would be mandatory. If 60 percent of the electorate voted to repeal a policy, it would be binding on the government.

A NOTE ON PARTIES

Political parties can either energize governance by giving it strong direction or deplete its capacity when competition turns to rigid ideological partisanship, as in the US today. As in all other realms, here, too, in the institutional design of governance much depends on what they contribute to balancing the body politic given cultural and historical conditions.

As we noted in the context of social networks, performance must ultimately match the claims of the common narrative a party presents to the public or authority and legitimacy will erode. But a shared narrative, not just shared information, is necessary to provide the patient allegiance required to allow policies for the long term to show fruition.

The means of constructing this narrative have different contexts in East and West. As Pan Wei[5] discussed in Chapter 3, the millennial heritage of China's "unitary rule" sees parties as expressions of "partial interests" that will splinter the unity of government for "all families." Since it has jettisoned "class struggle" as the core of its ideology to embrace all interests, the one-party rule of China's Communists has for all intents and purposes become the rule of "no party" – a return to the pragmatic roots of the Middle Kingdom's "institutional civilization."

Instead of external competition of many parties that can divide the body politic into "winners and losers," internal competition within the opaque confines of the Party allows different tendencies to contend with the aim of arriving at a consensus that is the disciplined basis for unified, decisive, and effective policy implementation. In this sense, the Party operates more like a private corporation. This is what happened when, fearing the return of Maoist politics, the populist impulses of the Chongqing Party chief, Bo Xilai, were reined in by the reassertion of collective leadership in the run-up to the transfer of power in China in 2012.

In the democratic West, competing parties can indeed mean "partial interests" battling each other at the expense of the common good, as we see in today's stiff partisan strife. When California Governor Jerry Brown was asked whether democracy was self-correcting, he quipped to us, "Only if we get rid of the party system."

Indeed, the American Founding Fathers saw a no-party system (not unlike the Confucians) as the best for the democracy they envisioned. As Richard Brookhiser writes in his political biography of James Madison:

> Madison and Jefferson certainly had no intention of founding a party, or "faction," as a political party was then often called. Although Madison thought factions were inevitable – "the latent cause of faction," he had written in Federalist #10, were "sown in the nature of man" – he also believed they were unjust. "By faction I understand a number of citizens . . . united and actuated by some common impulse of passion, or of interest, adverse to the rights of other citizens, or to the permanent and aggregate interests of the community." Factions were like germs – ubiquitous and unhealthy.[6]

But, as the historian Arthur Schlesinger Jr.[7] never tired of pointing out, mass political parties in the West are also the very mechanism for forging the consensus of a unified narrative out of diverse interests. The shaping of political will into a shared narrative by mass parties is what gives effective direction to the neutral apparatus of government.

Schlesinger championed competition between *two strong mass parties* in the American system precisely because one or the other could forge a governing consensus among a majority of voters. He believed that a weak two-party system or a proliferation of small parties would wreck that ability to govern. We can see Schlesinger's worry realized today in the United States as the weak party system yields to partisans instead of consensus-building centrists; we see in Israel the scourge of too many small parties where every fragile coalition government depends on its most extreme member in order to survive in power.

The conundrum we've discussed throughout this book also applies here: how to build a governing consensus while accommodating diverse voices. (One proposal in the European case study in Chapter 8 is to allow parties with less than 10 percent of the vote in the European Parliament to participate in debate, but not vote.)

Mass parties then, whether one or two, are consensus-building institutions. The greater the consensus a political system can produce, the more effective will be its governance. But for that consensus not to turn into complacency or stagnation, there must be a robust competition of ideas and viewpoints – either within a one-party system or through competition between or among parties.

Undeniably, the continuity of long one-party rule in a multi-party system – for example, the Liberal Democratic Party in Japan or the Social Democrats in Sweden – was responsible for raising those countries to the top ranks of global prosperity. Singapore's People's Action Party achieved its miracle over the past 50 years under the threat of "potential competition" from others. And, of course, China's awesome accomplishments over the past 30 years have resulted from one-party rule – but with internal competition for the top ranks of power based on proven accomplishment.

Lack of competition within a one-party system can lead to stagnation and decline, just as too much divisive competition and partisan "vetocracy" in multiparty systems can undermine the ability to build enough consensus to govern.

Noting that there is a debate in China today about the options of liberal democracy with many parties, a socialist democracy with one party, and a Confucian democracy with no parties, He Baogang[8] innovatively suggests that party competition can be scaled in varying manners.

There are two options. First, many parties could compete at the local level, where knowledge is more or less equal, but as the "public purpose is enlarged," moving from the village and county to the province and nation, less party competition is necessary because governance focuses on the whole instead of the particular.

Second, under different circumstances, the opposite scaling is also sensible. When facing practical local problems that rely on innovation instead of ideological frameworks about the overall direction of society, parties are not as necessary as consensus-building institutions. It is precisely at the higher levels, where "the public purpose is enlarged," that competition is most required.

SCALING GOVERNANCE

Where and how to involve, devolve, and delegate decisions under intelligent governance is bound up with this same discussion of scaling. Structures of governance rooted in past realities do not match the age of information and globalization, where citizens – if they choose to be informed – have access to the same knowledge as their governing class and when even the daily lives of small-town citizens are tied to global capital flows, energy and food supplies, integrated infrastructures, digital networks, migrant mobility, and shifting climate patterns.

Calibrating the appropriate jurisdictions for governance – decision-division – thus becomes the key challenge of governance. Should the same citizens who make decisions about local quality-of-life issues, from zoning and development to pollution, from sewage treatment to park landscaping or animal control, be expected to have a similar competence when it comes to regulating systemically critical global financial institutions or climate change, of which they are individually a miniscule part? At the same time, should national-scale plans for high-speed trains or subway lines run roughshod over citizens who might prefer to keep their trees in Stuttgart or Nanjing?

At the local and regional levels, where common sense is self-evident and problem-solving tends to be pragmatic, citizens can and should participate knowledgeably. At more distant levels – at the point of interaction and interdependence of many interests and influences – greater competence based on greater knowledge and experience is required because common sense is not so self-evident; good public policy is often at odds with what self-interest or special interest would dictate at the local or individual level.

When citizens are asked to decide on issues beyond their competence, ideology tends to take over from pragmatism. Then good governance goes astray.

There can be no one formula for how this calibration of powers and decision-division must be structured across societies with very different cultural and political contexts. What is important is institutional capacity that accommodates the need to balance interests, reconcile conflicts between different levels, and integrate local and global perspectives.

Clearly, there must be consent of the governed and accountability at all levels, but decision-discretion should be posited with those who are competent in their respective realm.

The point of this exercise in political imagination is not to propose a "one size fits all" model of governance. Rather, it is to show how the various tradeoffs between democratic accountability and knowledgeable meritocratic government might be structured.

In the succeeding chapters on California, the G-20, and Europe we report on our practical attempts to implement the elements of intelligent governance under actual political conditions.

6

Rebooting California's Dysfunctional Democracy

Introduction

California has long been the bellwether for the United States as a whole. Indeed, as the world's ninth largest economy and as home to Hollywood and Google, this outpost of creativity and innovation has continent-size influence with a cultural resonance that looms large in the global imagination.

Unfortunately, of late, California's role as a bellwether has taken on a decidedly negative cast. Where once Californians dreamed of building a society that matched the magnificence of the state's landscape, in recent years its citizens have settled instead for mountains of debt, disappearing jobs, D+ schools, greater public spending for prisons than higher education, and an outdated, crumbling infrastructure that emerging economies like China put to shame.

Where will California and America as a whole be two decades from now if we don't find a way for democratic societies to break out of the paralysis that is leading us from an era of promise to a trajectory of demise?

Every college freshman, entrepreneur, homeowner, new immigrant, or retiree in California has shared the sinking feeling that the future the state was once so famously said to be ahead of is passing them by. Facing daunting deficits after years of political gridlock, California has come in the minds of many to epitomize the crisis of democratic governance spreading across the West from Athens to Washington.

But, true to form as the land where second acts are possible, California seems be finally to reaching a tipping point and is preparing to come back. Once again it is ahead of the curve of the rest of the country.

Despite the successful recall election of a governor in 2003 and the concerted efforts of political leaders in the years since, Californians have come to realize that the real challenge is not so much replacing elected officials as fixing a system that is itself broken. As a result of this experience, the opportunity for the serious reform of California's governance process has opened up.

Since 2007, Californians have voted for open primaries, redistricting by citizen commission, and a simple majority vote on budgets – all with the aim of ending partisan paralysis in the legislature. And, by a huge margin, they voted for a clean energy future less dependent on foreign oil by protecting California's landmark climate change law from being overturned.

In 2010, the Nicolas Berggruen Institute (NBI) added a new set of voices to this growing movement by establishing the Think Long Committee for California, a high-powered group of eminent citizens with broad experience in public affairs, labor, and business financed with an initial $20 million to fight the requisite political campaigns for structural change. The name of the Committee itself implied its main objective: to introduce a depoliticized, nonpartisan, and long-term agenda as a corrective to the partisan rancor and short-term,

special-interest political culture that has come to dominate California political life.

The Committee ranges from two former secretaries of
state, George Shultz and Condoleezza Rice, to Clinton
economic advisor Laura Tyson; from Eric Schmidt of
Google to former Yahoo! and Warner Bros chief Terry
Semel, to former assembly speakers Bob Hertzberg
and Willie Brown and former state treasurer Matt
Fong, former UC Regents chair Gerry Parsky, former
California Supreme Court Justice Ron George, philan-
thropist Eli Broad, labor leader Maria Elena Durazo,
and anti-poverty advocate Antonia Hernández.

At our first meeting at Google headquarters in October
2010, then-Governor Arnold Schwarzenegger shared
the table with Gray Davis, the governor he ousted in the
2003 recall. The Committee has since worked closely
as well with Governor Jerry Brown, who returned to
the statehouse after two terms as governor in the late
1970s and early 1980s. The group is advised by the two
former state directors of finance, one a Republican and
one a Democrat, as well as the former chief economic
forecaster for the state.

After deliberating for a year in monthly sessions,
usually held at the Googleplex in Mountain View,
California, the group released its *Blueprint to Renew
California*[1] in November 2011.

Even as the dispiriting gridlock continued to grip
Sacramento, and as the so-called "supercommittee" of
the US Congress convened to figure a way out of the
nation's fiscal crisis failed to reach consensus, this group
of dedicated Californians succeeded in breaking out of
the untenable status quo. Putting politics aside, they
were able to bridge philosophical divides and agree to
a bipartisan plan to reboot California's dysfunctional
democracy.

Unlike many other piecemeal reform efforts over recent years, the Think Long Committee's plan seeks to modernize California's system of governance by installing a new civic software that follows the basic approach of "intelligent governance" outlined in this book: devolve, involve, and decision-division. We propose decentralizing power to the local level, on the one hand, while, on the other, creating greater capacity for depoliticized deliberation at the state level that incorporates a long-term perspective in governance.

Our integrated set of recommendations range from common-sense practices such as a "rainy day" reserve fund to multiyear budgeting; two-year legislative sessions with one year dedicated to oversight; K-12 school reform; aligning the skills and educational outcomes of California's master plan educational institutions with the needs of our cutting-edge industry; and speeding up regulatory approval to foster job creation.

But the core of our proposal has three parts:

Local empowerment (devolve and involve): Decision-making responsibilities and resources would be returned where appropriate from Sacramento to localities and regions where the real economy functions and government is closer to the people – and thus more responsive, flexible, and accountable. By helping to cover the costs of devolving public safety from the state to the counties, our plan will also help reduce the high costs associated with prisons.

The Think Long plan would dedicate new revenues annually to counties for public safety and as block grants to cities for infrastructure and other locally determined uses. Counties would be empowered to seek "waivers" from state rules and mandates to more flexibly pursue locally devised "strategic action plans," thus more actively engaging the grass roots. Labor, health, and environmental standards are exempt.

A depoliticized deliberative council (decision-division): An independent watchdog would be created for the long-term public interest as a counterbalance to the short-term mentality and special-interest political culture that dominate Sacramento.

This impartial and nonpartisan Citizens' Council for Government Accountability, composed of eminent citizens with expertise and experience in California affairs, would be tasked with both foresight and oversight responsibilities, deliberating on the "big picture" issues of the state and making recommendations to ensure that the public's long-term priorities are met. As a non-political quality control body, the Citizens' Council will ensure that California taxpayers get their "return on investment" through excellence in education, world-class infrastructure, a sustained quality of life, opportunities for good jobs, and the strengthening of a vibrant middle class through boosting the state's competitiveness in today's global economy.

Critically, the Council would be empowered to place its proposals directly on the public ballot as initiatives for public approval. We will discuss this Council in greater detail below.

A modern broad-based tax system (financing the future): California's tax system would be updated to mirror the real composition of its modern service and information economy and provide a stable, broad-based tax system that is sustainable over the long term.

The ideologically rigid will have a hard time putting the Think Long proposal in any box since it is a pragmatic response to the state's predicament. The essence of the bipartisan compromise involves expanding the sales tax to the service sector – not now taxed, despite the fact that is comprises half of California's $2 trillion economy – while at the same time reducing personal income taxes across the board in keeping with the state's historically progressive tax structure. This combination would generate $10 billion in new revenues annually, apportioned to pay down the state's wall of debt, fund K-12 schools and higher education, especially the University of California, and finance devolution to localities.

Over the coming years, the Think Long Committee will seek to implement this integrated set of reforms by placing constitutional and statutory amendments on initiative ballots for a public vote and by working directly with the governor and legislature where possible.

New Innovations in Democratic Governance

Like the convening of the Think Long Committee itself, the group's proposals with respect to governance seek to integrate more knowledge-based consensus-building capacity into the one-person-one-vote system through a combination of (a) deliberative polling (educating the voters); (b) reform of the initiative process and; (c) the establishment of the Citizens' Council (directly offering voters policy recommendations for their approval after thorough deliberation by a select body with experience and expertise). In short, we have tried to advance toward a *knowledgeable democracy* with elements of *accountable meritocracy*.

Deliberative Polling

In the summer of 2011, the Think Long Committee joined with another reform group, California Forward, to sponsor a weekend-long deliberative poll of 412 voters chosen on a random scientific basis to contemplate and debate changes in the way the state is governed.

The results of that poll, which indicatively represented the electorate at large, informed the drafting of the Government Performance and Accountability Act (GPAA),[2] a constitutional amendment that will go before voters in an upcoming ballot. Provisions of that initiative include a "pay-go" requirement for legislation (the legislature must show where the revenues or offsetting cuts will come from for new spending or tax credits), performance-based budgeting on two-year cycles with oversight review, and enabling more flexibility for county governments to make their own decisions by obtaining waivers from state mandates.

Initiative Reform

The mechanisms of direct democracy in California – the initiative (making laws), referendum (amending or nullifying laws), and recall (of public officials) provisions of the Constitution – were once heralded as the hallmarks of progressive government.[3] Under Governor Hiram Johnson, the state adopted the Swiss system of popular initiatives in 1914 as part of a series of reforms to give the public a way to challenge the railroad barons and large landowners who controlled state government.

While the initiative process was used sparingly until the 1970s, it became thereafter the chief battleground of state politics, nearly a "fourth branch" of government. Because of the high costs of gathering qualifying signatures and waging media campaigns in such a large state (usually in the tens of millions of dollars), this venue of the people has too often been subverted by special interests for their own ends or captured by ideological zealots who exploit short-term populist sentiments to advance their agenda.

As Andreas Kluth wrote in the *Economist* in its April 23, 2011 issue:

> The initiative culture as it exists in California today may resemble James Madison's worst nightmare. Passions are inflamed rather than cooled. Confrontation replaces compromise as minority factions (special interests) battle one another with rival initiatives. In 2009, Ronald George, at the time California's chief justice, worried publicly about the effect on liberty: "Has the voter initiative now become the tool of the very types of special interests it was intended to control, and an impediment to the effective functioning of a true democratic process?"[4]

The Think Long Committee's reforms on initiatives thus involve providing more information and analysis to voters about the various propositions than the 100 or so words allowed on the ballot summary written by the attorney general. They further involve mandating transparency on who is funding the proponents and opponents of a given measure. The proposed reforms would also revert California's system to the original Swiss process in which the proponents of initiatives are required to negotiate with the representative legislature so they can act on issues without going to a public ballot. Failing agreement, both the legislature's and the proponent's initiative would appear on the ballot side by side. By presenting alternatives, the process becomes more deliberative and less prone to special-interest manipulation; it would become more collaborative and less adversarial, restoring the balance between representative and direct democracy.

The Citizens' Council

The most innovative and far-reaching proposal of the Think Long governance reforms – the Citizens' Council for Government Accountability – would improve on California's unique mix of representative and direct democracy through the establishment of a depoliticized deliberative body that checks and balances both.

As noted in Figure 6.1 in brief, the Council would be a deliberative body tasked with foresight and oversight. It would ferret out waste and poor performance in state government while promoting the long-term priorities of the public: jobs, excellence in education, a clean environment, world-class infrastructure, and the fiscal health of state finances.

Although the council of 13 members would be

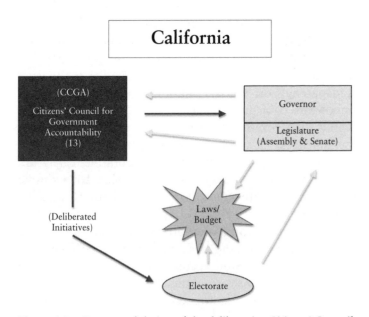

Figure 6.1   Conceptual design of the deliberative Citizens' Council (courtesy of Alexander Gardels)

appointed for six-year terms by the governor (nine members) and legislative leaders (four members) under procedures that would ensure its independence, any policies it might propose must be approved by the voters. Empowered to evaluate initiative proposals as well as place initiatives directly on the ballot on behalf of the public interest, the council would short-circuit the influence of special-interest money that has come to dominate the politics of propositions.

Working with the California state auditor, it would also possess subpoena power to audit spending, review programs, and recommend "sunsetting" of laws to make sure that taxpayers get what they are paying for.

To help ensure its constitutional integrity, the council idea was formulated with the prudent advice of Ron George, the chief justice of the California Supreme Court for 15 years and a member of the Think Long Committee.

Reporting on the Council proposal, the *Economist* predicted that "the next few years in California might see perhaps the liveliest debate about freedom and governance since Federalists and Anti-Federalists argued in 1787–88 about whether or not to ratify America's new constitution. Lovers of democracy and liberty everywhere still study that old debate. Now they will also pay attention to California's, for it will provide lessons for everyone."[5]

It is useful here to rehearse the arguments in our public campaign for the Citizens' Council because they reveal the points of contention that arise when proposing the introduction of meritocratic elements of governance in a democratic culture that distrusts delegation of authority.

Because of their limited terms, legislators generally lack both the time and incentives either for devising a long-term agenda or for performance review of the policies they put in place, "sunsetting" of laws, or follow-through. Since they are in office for only a short period, there is little accountability other than to the special interests that sponsor them, the lobbyists that influence them.

At one time, such a big-picture, long-term role was played by the California Senate as an "upper house" like the US Senate, based on geographical instead of population representation. Since 1968, however, the Senate and the Assembly in California have duplicated each other's role with overlapping districts based on population. This has meant a necessarily narrow focus by legislators on the particular, short-term concerns of local constituents rather than on the state as a whole.

The point of the Council is to create an institutional counterbalance to the short-term, special-interest political culture of Sacramento as well as to its narrow constituent focus.

Like the rest of the United States, California needs a long-term strategic agenda if it is going to prosper in the decades ahead. The legislature is just not disposed or equipped to fulfill this task.

Questions about the accountability and the legitimacy of the Council have naturally been raised. In response, certain safeguards have been instituted. First, the Council would be appointed by the state's democratically elected officials. Second, what it might propose can go into effect only if approved by the public at the ballot box. Third, council members can be removed for corruption or malfeasance by the Senate.

Some pundits have quipped that the Council would be being granted "king's power." Others have called it "A House of Lords." This is nonsense. What king, or hereditary nobility, ever had to go to the public at large in a general election to approve or reject their policies?

The Council meets the criteria of both legitimacy and accountability: its members would be selected by democratically elected representatives of the people, and its proposals would be approved or rejected through the direct democracy of the initiative system.

The reason the Council would be appointed instead of elected is to insulate it from the same short-term, special-interest influences that result from electoral campaigns.

While the Council's legitimacy must necessarily derive from appointment by elected officials, Council members would be appointed in a way – with strict limitations on political contributions they can make to the appointing officials and with terms that cross electoral cycles – that would ensure their independence and long-range perspective while avoiding the patronage, cronyism, and partisanship that has immobilized state governance.

Another concern has been voiced that, because the governor would have the majority of appointments to the Council, the body would do his bidding.

This, however, is a structural proposal for governance that is meant to be in place for decades, and not just for one governor or another. The staggered six-year appointments across political cycles would result in a mix of different gubernatorial appointments over time, as is the case with the California Supreme Court, the Regents of the University of California, the Public Utilities Commission, and the Coastal Commission.

The logic of giving the governor the most appointments is that, though the legislature represents specific constituencies, the governor represents the "general will" because he is elected statewide and is thus best positioned to select Council members accordingly.

However, one way to remedy this concern is to follow the precedent of the appointment process for the Commission on Judicial Performance in the California Constitution. This would allow for five of the governor's selections to be appointed for an initial two-year term and then be eligible for appointment to the full six-year term after that tenure. The other four members would be appointed to the full six-year terms. In this way, a staggered schedule would be set in place giving future governors as well as the current governor a key role.

Rightly suspicious of waste in government, some worry the Council would be just another bureaucratic layer between the public and getting results from government. The Council, however, would not be an agency of bureaucrats, but a body of citizens – paid on a *per diem* basis and bound by strict conflict-of-interest rules – charged with the responsibility of being a deliberative watchdog for the public interest. This body would be a quality-control body that will make sure the taxpaying public gets a long-term "return on its investment."

Despite the reality that the Council would truly empower citizens by being a nonpartisan advocate for the long-term public interest, some fear it would weaken the public's right to recourse. Yet, it is misleading to argue that the initiative process as it exists today provides a means of recourse for the ordinary citizen. Although historically the initiative process has played a key role in giving the public a direct voice in governance, the mounting costs of signature gathering and media have led to the process being captured by special interests and ideological causes pursuing short-term aims. It is these organized interests that have usurped citizens' power. The Council would recover that power for citizens.

All citizens would be welcomed to submit proposals for initiatives to the Council.

Unless we remove money from the politics of ballot propositions, this proposal provides the public with the best option for California's future because it will be an advocate for the public at the ballot box and a trusted guide for an electorate busy with family and work to sort through the thicket of spin and special interests that initiative campaigns have mostly become.

The Council may in fact be the public's best safeguard of the initiative process.

The Next Step

As devolution and "realignment" of responsibilities and revenues to localities proceed over the coming years in California and the state government assumes a leaner and more strategic role, it would make sense in time to make two further structural changes. First, the current state Senate, which, as we explained, has become a purely representative, non-deliberative body like the state Assembly, would be replaced with the Citizens' Council for Government Accountability as a genuine deliberative "upper house." Second, the representative districts of the Senate and Assembly would be merged into one lower house with a stepped form of elections to promote more grass-roots citizens' engagement.

When the structure of state governance was established, California adopted a bicameral legislature – a Senate and an Assembly – on the federal model of a Senate and House of Representatives.

Yet, the purpose of a Senate and House at the federal level is to balance representation based on population with representation based on the 50 state jurisdictions,

139

with two senators each, whose terms are longer to encourage deliberation.

This arrangement, however, makes little sense at the state level, where both the Senate and the Assembly duplicate representation by population, only with different-sized districts drawn on an arbitrary basis.

Conceivably, the present Senate (40 members) and Assembly (80 members) would be combined into one nonpartisan legislative chamber with 120 representatives and a strong committee structure. This would allow the size of the districts to be smaller (300,000 or so instead of 1 million citizens), thus making legislators more responsive and accountable by bringing them closer to their constituents. Districts would be held to a population of 300,000, with more seats added as the population grows.

Moreover, following the stepped system in our general template, each district of 300,000 could be divided into six neighborhood councils of 50,000 each. Each of the six neighborhoods would elect one delegate to the district council. That council would in turn elect the representative for that district to the state legislature.

This new civic software would be more efficient, less redundant, and less contentious, also greatly reducing the overhead costs of two houses. It would dampen the influence of money in politics (necessitated by fundraising for media in large jurisdictions) by limiting the population size of districts and curbing the power of lobbyists who play one house off against the other. Above all, it would close the distance between the represented and the representative and involve local citizens more meaningfully in setting the rules that govern their lives.

Replacing the Senate with a genuine upper house with deliberative responsibilities would further balance the short-term and local nature of constituency representation of the lower house, as historically intended.

Change along these lines would shift California toward a modern system of governance that has the capacity for decisive action, reflects the complexity and diversity of its population and economy, and is more suited to the challenges and opportunities of the 21st century than the one inherited from the time of ranches and railroad barons.

Above all, the checks, balances, and incentives of this new civic software would imbue governance with a public-interest political culture that replaces the rancor of polarization with the nonpartisan spirit of pragmatism and the long-range perspective associated with the great builders of the state in the 1950s and 1960s – Republican Governor Earl Warren and Democratic Governor Pat Brown – who laid the foundations in the post-World War II era for the prosperity and quality of life that California enjoyed for decades.

If Californians embrace such an approach, they could have a fiscally sound government that can weather the ups and downs of the business cycle and foster the high-wage jobs linked to California's cutting-edge industries, from bio-tech to information technology to clean energy. Upward mobility could be ensured through excellent schools with affordable higher education, accessible to all Californians, that provide the innovative and highly skilled workers who are key to building competitive new industries. Environmentally friendly, livable cities that use energy and water smartly could be a model for the world.

Despite its current travails, California is rightly known for its can-do creativity. If that can be turned toward the task of good governance, all Californians will be empowered to get back to the future with the government they want and deserve.

Lessons of the California Experience

If the reforms proposed by the Think Long Committee can take hold, California is well positioned in other respects to face the coming era. Its fundamentals are strong: a diverse population of hard-working immigrants from everywhere, an entrepreneurial energy linked to venture capital resources unmatched elsewhere in the world, world-class universities, abundant agriculture, a temperate climate, and magnificent natural landscape. The most vibrant new industries on the planet – represented by companies from Genentech to Intel, Google, and Facebook, to a wide array of clean energy companies – have emerged in recent years from this fertile California environment.

Yet, despite what appears to be a growing openness to reform on the part of the public, the obstacles to change we have encountered remain daunting.

The first lesson is that good policy can be bad politics – and bad policy is sometimes good politics. This is at the root of the incapacity of the one-person-one-vote system to self-correct absent the counterbalance of a deliberative body that takes into account the long-term consequences of the quick fixes that popular democracy favors.

In a context of deep cuts in education and social programs, the temptation of politics as usual is to look for a solution that polls well instead of fixing the state for the long term. This is precisely what happened in 2012 when Governor Brown, the California Federation of Teachers, and other groups, fueled by the 99 percent movement, sought to close the state's funding gap by taxing the easiest target – the rich. They did so because it is far more politically viable to tax "others" than the broad middle class that makes up most of the voting public, even though, as our Think Long Committee rec-ommended, a modern broad-based sales tax on services in which everyone pays slightly more would stabilize revenues for years to come.

While there is much to be said, and which we have said in this book, about the need to stem growing ine-quality, California is already perched on a narrowly vol-atile tax base where the top 5 percent of earners account through income and capital gains taxes for 67 percent of revenues. As we have explained, the boom and bust of the budget cycle that results from this narrow reliance means that programs funded in a good year (for exam-ple when Google or Facebook go public and capital gains skyrocket) simply have to be drastically cut when there is an economic downturn and top-end revenues drop dramatically. The situation is made worse by the absence of a "rainy day" savings fund – which the same groups oppose precisely because it would curb spending in good years.

The end result is a dysfunctional system that gener-ates perpetual deficits, drives up borrowing costs, and deprives the state of a growing source of future revenue needed to invest in precisely those public goods – higher education and infrastructure – that are the structural answer to growing inequality.

Others lessons of our effort to bring "intelligent gov-ernance" to California could easily be lifted from the texts of political scientists like Francis Fukuyama or economic theorists like Mancur Olson whom we have mentioned before several times in this book.

In its short history, California has, in the broadest sense, followed the same trajectory of the rise and politi-cal decay of systems of governance as seen in the ups and downs of China's millennia-long experience or that of the Ottoman Empire that Francis Fukuyama documents in his magisterial *The Origins of Political Order*. In each case, formerly robust institutions of good governance eventually corroded because they failed to adjust to new conditions or succumbed to the relentless resurgence of what Fukuyama calls "patrimonialization" – that is, the dominance of special interests over the general interests of the public.

As Fukuyama writes:

> Institutions are created in the first place to meet the competitive challenges of a particular environment. . . . [W]hen the original conditions leading to the creation or adoption of an institution change, the institution fails to adjust quickly to meet the new circumstances. The disjunction in rates of changes between institutions and the external environment then accounts for political decay and deinstitutionalization.[6]

This has certainly been true of California. The Golden State rose to economic prominence during the post-World War II years when it became the thriving outpost of the American empire's vast military-industrial complex and when cheap energy fueled the state's sprawling growth. In those days, a growing middle class that still saved more than it consumed was willing and able to finance infrastructure investments in the future, from a quality education system that included the expansion of the University of California to the state's famed network of freeways to the system of canals that brought water from the snowy Sierra Nevada peaks and wet north to the parched south.

With the advent of a mass consumer culture in the 1960s and the commensurate emphasis on the single-family home instead of the public weal as the locus of the California Dream, the real-estate bubble that finally burst in sub-prime mortgage crisis of 2008–9 began to build. Along with that now burst bubble came the end, for the foreseeable future, of a decades-long boom in construction jobs.

Proposition 13 in 1979 marked the revolt of the homeowner/taxpayer, which significantly deprived the state of its most stable source of financing for local services and education by severely limiting property taxes. Even as the population doubled and immigration from Mexico swelled, the state could never make up the difference, going deeply into debt just to maintain operations, much less invest in the future.

The military-industrial complex withered with the end of the Cold War. Easy credit dried up with the financial crash as the housing market collapsed. With the rapid growth of China and India, global energy demand is conjoining with Middle East turmoil to end the era of cheap fuel.

Yet, despite increasing acceptance of the need for reform, Californians have remained in denial, as if they were historically entitled to a future as promising as the past has been.

The resurgence of special interests who capture the state, as Fukuyama argues, meanwhile eats away at that future. In this, as we have pointed out elsewhere, his argument is similar to that of Mancur Olson in his classic 1982 book, *The Rise and Decline of Nations: Economic Growth, Stagflation, and Social Rigidities*.[7]

Using rational choice theory, Olson argued that organized special interests, whether labor unions or business associations, assert their interests more effectively in a democracy than individual citizens because the return on their activism is higher as a collective body than it is for the diaspora of unorganized individual citizens – the general public. Thus, public employee unions

145

can garner hefty pension deals or business lobbyists can garner hefty tax breaks, or avoid taxation. These interest groups thus become the primary "stakeholders" in the public budget, accreting like barnacles onto state government.

Any California reform effort, as was true for the Think Long Committee, runs directly up against these "stakeholders" who have taken the state government hostage. Especially with term limits on legislators, their lobbyists are more a permanent presence in Sacramento than the people's representatives, and, because they sponsor the election campaigns, elected officials are largely beholden to them.

This situation is compounded by the initiative process in California. Once the means of public recourse, initiatives, as former California Supreme Court Justice Ron George mentioned above, as often as not have become a battleground of well-funded special interests fighting each other.

When deciding which issues to take to the public ballot, the main consideration of the Think Long Committee was who would oppose it and how much they might spend to defeat reform that threatened their interests. If you want to raise revenues, the anti-tax lobby will spend $40 million against you. The huge entertainment conglomerates based in California will likely spend whatever it takes to stop a 5 percent services sales tax on tickets for movies or theme parks, revealing their societal priority of amusement over education.

If you want to reform K-12 schools, the California Teachers Association will spend $50 million to keep teacher tenure and avoid evaluation. If you want to close the tax loopholes on commercial property, the large land and commercial real estate corporations will spend $100 million to stop you. If you want to impose an oil severance tax, the large oil companies will spend what it takes to prevent that from happening

But it is not only the special interests that abuse the initiative process. So does the public, which, through this tool of direct democracy, has contributed significantly to California's political decay. Mainly, this is because the public irresponsibly mandates spending which it then refuses to pay for with sufficient taxation. Locked-in spending and locked-out revenues are at the core of the state's fiscal crisis.

The most egregious example of this was the "Three Strikes" initiative, which required imprisonment after a third felony conviction, and mandatory doubling of the sentence on the second "strike." While this understandably appealing attempt to improve public safety was overwhelmingly approved at the polls, no commensurate spending plan to build more prisons was included. As a result, a decade after the passage of this law by initiative, the US Supreme Court, in May 2011, ordered the release of 36,000 prisoners from California jails because overcrowding violated their human rights.[8]

As already noted, Proposition 13 is another case in point. By limiting the property tax collections by localities to 2 percent of the assessed value of their homes, California homeowners were able to escape increasingly burdensome taxation. Yet, this deprived government of the requisite resources for education and public safety services, never yet to have been replaced.

The point of representative democracy was to create deliberative bodies that would take into account the longer-term ramifications of their decisions. The inherent short-sighted nature of direct democracy, which has tied California's finances in knots, was exactly what America's Founding Fathers, such as James Madison and Alexander Hamilton, in their wisdom, sought to avoid.

The California experience not only suggests that good governance must guard against the age-old onset of political decay as a result of rigidity in the face of changed conditions and repatrimonialization. It also warns against a common assumption that more direct democracy ought to be part and parcel of the knowledge society. Good governance requires checks and balances not only on government, but on the public as well.

7

The G-20

Global Governance from Summits to Subnational Networks

Introduction

"Our interdependent world means that our problems are no longer just problems we share in common," former British Prime Minister Gordon Brown has said, "but are global, interwoven between countries, and only concerted action across continents can effectively tackle them."[1]

For better and for worse, the G-20 has emerged as the key embryonic institution of global governance that Gordon Brown is calling for because it reflects the radical power shift underway owing to the rise of the emerging powers. Including Europe, Japan, and the US along with the likes of China, Brazil, Mexico, India, South Africa, and Turkey among its 20 members, it is, in effect, the mechanism of adjustment from Globalization 1.0 to 2.0.*

While the advanced economies are increasingly unable to provide global public goods – such as open trade,

---

* Except where noted, all quotes and discussion points in this section are taken from the notes of a meeting of the 21st Century Council held in New York on March 26–7, 2011.

149

stable financial flows, or mitigation of climate change – on their own, the emerging economies are not yet able to do so.

Unlike the old G-7 – which were all democratic, free market economies – the G-20 brings together a broad mix of civilizations and economic and political systems, from the Western liberal democracies to China's market-Leninist/neo-Confucian order to Turkey's secular state ruled by an Islamic party. Figuring out how to co-operatively govern this new interdependence of plural identities – in which the economic convergence *and* cultural divergence of Globalization 2.0 are taking place simultaneously – will be an unprecedented challenge. Never before has there been a truly a multi-polar global civilization with no single hegemon, or bloc of powers, obliged by their own self-interest to provide global public goods whose value also accrues to others.

That challenge is compounded further by the bottom-up ideology of political awakenings across the globe with restive publics clamoring from the grass roots for a say in the rules that govern their lives.

If legitimacy is a function of local proximity, as Pascal Lamy has often said, how do we square the challenge of making the distant G-20 the trusted mechanism of a peaceful adjustment of the world power shift with the now regular eruptions of grass-roots discontent of the Occupy Wall Steet movement, the Arab youth in Tahrir Square, the *indignados* in Madrid, the Moscow populist bloggers, or the angry villagers in Wukan or Haimen in China's southern Guangdong province?

As we've discussed in the other contexts, is it possible to further enhance the effectiveness of global governance at the G-20 level and at the same time empower more proximate polities through a combination of devolving, involving, and decision-division? In the mega-urban planet of the 21st century, will networks or subnational leagues of city-state-like arrangements once again, as in the Middle Ages, become the locus of a *modus vivendi* that reconciles the global and the local?

To help answer these questions both in theory and in practice, in 2011 we established the 21st Century Council as a kind of "shadow G-20." The group includes former world leaders from both the advanced and emerging economies, top global thinkers, and key "disrupters" from the world of social networking media.

Many of the former political leaders on the Council all have historic transformations under their belt: Mexico's Ernesto Zedillo and Spain's Felipe González shepherded the democratic transition in their countries; Germany's Gerhard Schroeder and Brazil's Fernando Henrique Cardoso turned their respective economies around and made their countries among the most competitive in the world; China's Zheng Bijian, the former permanent vice-president of the powerful Central Party School and author of China's "peaceful rise" doctrine, drafted the famous report for Deng Xiaoping's "southern tour" to reboot the "reform and opening up" policies in 1992; and Britain's Gordon Brown successfully managed the global response to the financial crisis at the London G-20 meeting in 2009. After leaving office, Nicolas Sarkozy also joined the group. Other leaders in the group include Singapore's former Foreign Minister George Yeo, Pakistan's former Prime Minister Shaukaut Aziz, and Africa's most honest statesman, former Botswanian President Festus Mogae. Former US Treasury Secretary Larry Summers and former Canadian Prime Minister Paul Martin, who together founded the G-20 in 1999, are also members.

Global thinkers range from Pascal Lamy (who also

heads the World Trade Organization) to economists Raghuram Rajan and Nouriel Roubini as well as top bond trader Mohamed El-Erian and former IMF chief Rodrigo de Rato, along with Chinese venture capitalists Fred Hu and Eric X. Li. Nobel laureates on the group include Amartya Sen, Michael Spence, Joseph Stiglitz, and Ahmed Zewail. Also involved are Fareed Zakaria, Francis Fukuyama, John Gray, Alain Minc, Kishore Mahbubani, and futurist Peter Schwartz.

"Disrupters" include Google's Eric Schmidt, YouTube's Chad Hurley, Twitter's Jack Dorsey, blogging pioneer Arianna Huffington, and e-Bay founders Jeff Skoll and Pierre Omidyar.

Each year the group informally advises the G-20 chair leading up to the annual summit. It meets twice a year – once on the eve of the summit to release its communiqué and recommendations and then once separately.

In 2011 we met in Paris to advise French President Nicolas Sarkozy at the height of the euro crisis, then in May 2012 in Mexico City when the G-20 was hosted by President Felipe Calderón. The group has also arranged to meet the new leadership in China after the transfer of power in the fall of 2012. India and Russia are next on the agenda.

The hope of the 21st Century Council is that it can contribute, both conceptually and practically, to establishing a new equilibrium in the era of Globalization 2.0 through its own network of personal relationships as well as its direct influence on the leaders of the G-20. One of the most important roles it can play when "present at the creation" of the next world order is helping define the relationship between a rising China and a West on the wane after centuries in the driver's seat.

The G-20

Convergence of Interests

For years, the West has been calling on a rising China to become a "responsible stakeholder" in the global system. China's response has been to hold back from taking any initiative, not only because the global system it would be buying into was historically established on Western terms, but also because of its laser-like focus on developing its domestic economy.

However, the combination of China's symbolic coming-out party at the 2008 Olympics, its robust resilience in the wake of the financial crisis emanating from Wall Street – the heart of the global system – and its ascendance to the No. 2 economy in the world has prompted the country's leaders to now rise to the challenge on their own terms.

Those terms have been spelled out by Zheng Bijian, the doyen of the Central Party School, confidant of China's leaders, author some years ago of the "peaceful rise"[2] doctrine, and a key member of the 21st Century Council.

The new concept is to move from "peaceful rise" to "expand and deepen convergence of interests" and foster "communities of interest" globally, particularly with the United States, in a "pragmatic spirit." When there is an accumulation of converging interests," Zheng says, "there will be a solid foundation of common interests."

China's strategy for the first two decades of the 21st Century has been to "build a moderately prosperous society," Zheng notes. "Now half of this relatively independent historical period has passed" and, in order to improve the life of ordinary Chinese in "qualitative" instead of just "quantitative" terms, the next decade will have to be accomplished "in the context of interdependence."

153

Addressing both the need to reduce global imbalances and improve the people's lives "qualitatively," Zheng argues that "we must transform our economy from one mainly driven by external demand to one driven by both domestic and external demand, mainly domestic. China, a lower-middle income country, will move to an upper-middle income country at a faster pace."[3]

To achieve this will require "dialogue, consultations and coordination" with the rest of the world. To this end, Zheng has been in close conversation with US strategists Zbigniew Brzezinski and Henry Kissinger to define "ten points of convergence" between China and the West and how to build on them. He also delivered the keynote address at the October 2011 meeting of the 21st Century Council in Paris outlining his idea to the global leaders gathered there.

In order to "concretize" the idea of "a community of interests," Zheng proposes, for example, that the US and China join together to promote clean energy and "low-carbon" development in both countries. He also suggests that China should finance infrastructure development in the US, helping to create jobs and the foundation for US domestic growth even as China is shifting to more domestic consumption.

Critically, these are not just Zheng's ideas. They have been inscribed in the Communist Party Central Committee's 12th Five Year Plan for Economic and Social Development, China's roadmap for the future.[4] In a conversation with Michael Spence at a meeting of the China Development Forum, Wen Jiabao talked about the G-20 as the key forum to develop China's approach of "a convergence of interests" in order to build "a community of interests."

The G-20: Clothes without an Emperor

While the logical forum for promoting "a community of interests" on a global scale is the G-20, as Wen Jiabao suggested, it is so far a weak institution that needs bolstering. Just as the world's second largest economy is preparing to actively adapt to interdependence, the G-20, as Nouriel Roubini[5] argues, risks becoming the "G-Zero" – a forum of conflict instead of cooperation. At the Council's meeting in Paris, former US Vice-President Al Gore dismissed the G-20 as an ineffective body, calling it "clothes without an emperor," in a witty reference to the group photos of suited leaders taken at the end of each summit.

"We are now living in a G-Zero world," says Roubini, "one in which no single country or bloc of countries has the political and economic leverage – or the will – to drive a truly international agenda. The result will be intensified conflict on the international stage over vitally important issues such as macroeconomic coordination, financial regulatory reform, trade policy and climate change."[6] One might sensibly add that there will also be intensified conflict over energy and raw materials.

Despite this present lack of consensus, Roubini acknowledges that emergent crises have a way of forging a new consensus for action when issues of common interest become pressing. Gerhard Schroeder observes just such a shift over the past years within the European Union: Germany has come much closer to the French position of much tighter coordination of economic policies in Europe as a result of the enduring sovereign debt crisis. The same forces will be at play with respect to the G-20.

Pascal Lamy, director-general of the World Trade Organization – the most effective of all the extant institutions of global governance – makes Roubini's G-Zero point in the opposite way. The problem with the current institutions of global governance, he says, is that they only have "secondary legitimacy" as "assemblies of nation states." What they need to be effective is "primary legitimacy." That can only come by building up the "community of interests" (in Zheng's words), by bringing global governance "closer to citizens," particularly by employing social networking technology so that "citizens are inhabited by a sense of togetherness."[7] Needless to say, this is a long-term project.

Whether the civilization of the satellite, so to speak, can one day supplant the civilization of the soil as a means of creating common identities is one of the big question marks for the future. The passionate allegiance that is evident in virtual tribes suggests this can be a reality. And, indeed, Eric Schmidt and Jared Cohen of Google argue that such a parallel world of identities not associated with the soil is arising in cyberspace alongside the multi-polar world in physical space, adding yet another dimension to interdependence.

The great challenge, therefore, is how to move toward "a convergence of interests" when the executive committee of global governance – the G-20 – is beset by centrifugal tendencies instead of drawn toward unity. The success of any supranational body in achieving primary legitimacy must rest on the appropriate calibration of local characteristics and interests with global imperatives. The 21st century, as we've discussed throughout this book, is likely to be more local and global at the same time.

The historical stakes are high.

The futurist Peter Schwartz aptly asks whether the present period is more like 1910 than 1950. After World War II and the ascent of the US, global rules and institutions that provided "global public goods" in the mold of the American system were being established. In 1910, a series of shifting alliances based on interests ended up stumbling adrift into World War I when the assassination of Archduke Ferdinand ruptured the frail stability of the system.

Fernando Henrique Cardoso has also observed that, in history, any new regime of global governance is a consequence of "a consensus of the winners," as was the case with America and its allies in the wake of World War II. The problem today, he has said, is that "the old winners are beginning to lose and it is not yet fully clear to what extent the emerging economies are the winners. Who, then, will belong to the 'community of interests' proposed by Zheng Bijian? Who will establish the new rules and institutions and provide the global public goods?" The G-20, Cardoso suggested, might not be "ready for prime time. It could take 15 years."

Moreover, as Cardoso, Schroeder, Lamy, and others have suggested, building a new order today is a matter not only for nation-states, but also for subnational entities like the emerging megacity-regions as well as global civil society.

Global within the Local

Former IMF chief economist Raghuram Rajan proposes an answer to this challenge as global institutions build up to "primary legitimacy" over the longer term. "The role of multilateral bodies, such as the G-20 and the IMF, should not be to coordinate policies among countries but to *insert the international dimension into each country's domestic policy debate on reform* [author's emphasis]. It should also be to set reasonable rules of the game on financial regulation, cross-border capital flows and international bailouts."[8]

In other words, rather than, for example, focusing on summit agreements on currency exchange rates, indicators of surplus or deficits, or greenhouse gas mandates, the G-20 countries should engage in *domestically defined paths of reform that lead toward convergence* which take into account *the rapidly changing political, cultural, and structural realities of each nation-state.* This is the way to reconcile the local and the global.

Going the route of G-20 summitry alone, Rajan argues, will, in effect, produce the "G-Zero" result that Roubini warns about.

According to Rajan, for China, for example, a "domestically defined path of reform that leads toward convergence" would mean increasing wages; raising interest rates for household bank deposits; improving the delivery of health and educational services; raising corporate taxes and lowering subsidies on inputs such as energy and land; and investing in infrastructure to link poorer inland regions to the coasts.

A domestically defined path toward convergence for the United States, as Rajan sees it, would focus more on tailoring the skills and education of the US workforce to the jobs that are being created, rather than hankering after the old jobs eliminated by technology or overseas competition. This must include improving educational standards by measuring student performance, evaluating teachers' abilities, and increasing competition between schools.

For Rajan, the United States also needs a better social safety net, not only to reassure workers but also to ensure that slow recoveries do not result in frenetic, and ultimately excessive, stimulus spending aimed at creating jobs as quickly as possible.

While "domestically defined paths" to global solutions may work in some areas such as climate change, in the trade and financial realms Ernesto Zedillo argues that finding a way to address the global macroeconomic imbalances through coordinated policies at the summit level is the "litmus test" of the G-20. Rather than hope domestic governments take up their responsibilities, the G-20 should put a robust mechanism in place for coordination.

Believing that "peer review" by G-20 members of their own contribution to global imbalances is too weak, he would press for a more robust surveillance capacity of the International Monetary Fund to call out China on its overvalued currency or the US on its looming deficits, enhanced multilateral insurance against lack of credit availability in order to reduce the need to hold large quantities of reserves, and a renewed push to complete the Doha round of trade negotiations.

His experience at the World Trade Organization suggests to Pascal Lamy a fusion of Rajan's and Zedillo's approach that finds a proper combination among the localization of global issues, country endeavors that have to be peer reviewed, and international disciplines "the breach of which must have a cost."

To address the globally relevant issues, each dimension must be put in one of these "clusters."

Lamy believes the articulation of the various elements of global governance, including the United Nations system, can be further structured through a "triangle of coherence" that draws on the attributes of each.

"On one side of the triangle lies the G-20, replacing the former G-8 and providing political leadership, policy direction and coherence," Lamy says. "The second side of the triangle is the United Nations, which provides a framework for global legitimacy through accountability. On the third side lie member-driven international organizations providing expertise and specialized inputs, be they rules, policies or programs."

A Hybrid Model: Summits and Networks

Taking this analysis into account, the 21st Century Council gathering in Mexico City in May 2012 proposed a hybrid approach for the G-20 to provide global public goods.

First, summit agreements make sense on financial regulation, cross-border capital flows, and international bailouts bolstered by strong and independent "surveillance" of G-20 economies on practices that contribute to imbalances. Our recommendations here included the establishment of "two-track sherpas" (permanent and annual) to carry out and ensure the continuity of policies from summit to summit, organized through the "troika" of the immediate past, present, and future G-20 chairs, and the expansion of the Organization for Economic Cooperation and Development (OECD) to include the G-20 emerging economies. Among the tasks of the G-20 OECD would be to measure trade flows in a new way that takes into account contemporary global scattering of production (as in iPad manufacture, see Chapter 4) and its impact on trade and employment. Coordinated global policy on reducing imbalances must be based on an objective commonly shared analysis of the facts or it will lead to unnecessary tensions and conflict.

Second, a web of national and subnational networks should be fostered to provide global public goods – such as low-carbon growth to combat climate change – from below through "coalitions of the willing" working together to build up to a threshold of global change.

As proposed at the May 2012 G-20 meeting in Mexico, where President Calderón focused on "green growth," arrangements like the Clean Development Mechanism under the Kyoto Treaty could be bolstered. It is essentially a global "commodities exchange for carbon permits" that enables trading among national and subnational jurisdictions that already have or are planning a cap and trade system – such as California, Australia, Quebec, some European states and Chinese provinces. Ultimately, the resulting liquidity created by this exchange would encourage other jurisdictions to join.

A further idea we discussed was to link the R-20, or "regional 20," with the G-20 goals on climate change. The R-20 was founded by Arnold Schwarzenegger when he was California governor and its members range from the Gujarat State in India to the Gyeonggi Provincial Government in South Korea to Puglia in Italy. The idea is that, even if progress on climate change and clean energy is stymied at the level of global governance or the nation-state, the subnationals can still move ahead to build a critical mass from below.

Figure 7.1 illustrates a conceptual configuration of how summitry and networks might work together.

Aside from advising the G-20, the 21st Century Council has taken on projects where it can have a direct impact through its personal networks of relationships. One example is following up Zheng Bijian's argument for "building a community of interests" between the US and China, the core of the global economy, by encouraging direct foreign investment of China's surpluses into infrastructure and jobs in the United States – thus elegantly squaring the circle of trade and employment and staunching the rise of protectionist sentiments by showing that globalization can put people to work in the US as well as China.

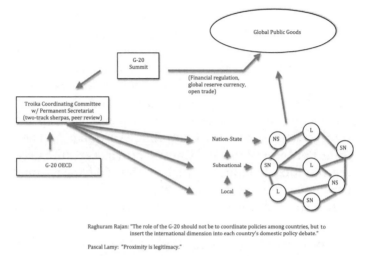

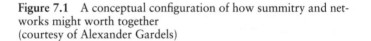

Raghuram Rajan: "The role of the G-20 should not be to coordinate policies among countries, but to insert the international dimension into each country's domestic policy debate."

Pascal Lamy: "Proximity is legitimacy."

Building a community from below, e.g. R20 Subnational Clean Energy Network

Figure 7.1 A conceptual configuration of how summitry and networks might worth together
(courtesy of Alexander Gardels)

When Xi Jinping visited California in February 2012, Governor Jerry Brown, speaking as one princeling to another (Brown's father was also governor; Xi's father was a top member of the Politburo), proposed that China might be able to help finance the state's planned $90 billion bullet train system as well as invest in "plug and play" zones* in the more impoverished, high-jobless areas of California such as the Central Valley and Riverside County.[9]

There is a certain elegant symmetry in this latter endeavor as well. When Brown visited Guangdong province in the early 1980s,[10] just after his first terms

---

* This refers to special economic zones pre-permitted for all the various local, state, and federal regulations so that business can just "plug in" and start up or expand.

in the statehouse, he was hosted by Xi Jinping's father, Xi Zhongxun, who at that time was governor of Guangdong. Xi senior, an intimate of Deng Xiaoping, was the mastermind behind China's new experiment at the time with the "special economic zone" in Shenzhen. He was seeking investment from the United States!

Through its network of contacts in California on the Think Long Committee and ties in China to the top officials of the China Investment Corporation and Zheng Bijian, the 21st Century Council was able to facilitate the advance of these projects.

This project is but one example of how a "global civil society" group like the 21st Century Council, along with business and government at all levels, can contribute to resolving the divergence/convergence and global/local contradictions of today's power shift.

Applying the "devolve, involve, and decision-division" paradigm of intelligent governance can help build the "primary legitimacy" the G-20 will need to address the new global challenges.

The alternative is a power vacuum, drift, and then the risk of destructive conflict. There is no higher priority for global governance than doing all one can to make sure the present is more like 1950 than 1910.

8

Europe

Political Union and the Democratic Deficit

The historic project of European integration has more than stalled. It is at an existential impasse.

Europe's sovereign debt crisis was triggered by imbalances that came about because the single currency created deep economic interdependence without the capacity for common governance. What the German writer Hans Magnus Enzensberger[1] calls the "gentle monster" in Brussels meddled where it had no business – for example, dictating the length of condoms – while not meddling where it should have – monitoring the fiscal and competitive conditions among member states. It crept toward micromanaging the social life of its members while leaving the macroeconomy to work itself out.

There are now only two choices: disintegration by moving back to the nation-state without even a common currency; or moving ahead toward some form of full federal political union – albeit, in our view, through a strong, *but limited* state that leaves the diversity of Europe undiminished.

In a sense, Europe faces the same set of challenges as the G-20: how to share sovereignty in a way that also promotes national well-being in the long term, and thus

garners the support of the public. Just like the G-20 –
and just as with systems of governance within nation-
states – greater authority is required at higher levels for
the coordination and management of interdependence
at the systemic level, even as national and local identities gain a greater voice at their appropriate levels of
competence.

The Nicolas Berggruen Institute Council on the Future
of Europe has sought to address these issues by gathering together a small group of Europe's most eminent
and experienced political figures to debate and design
the institutions that would govern a federal Europe and
then plot a path forward, step by step.

The group includes Marek Belka (Poland), former
prime minister; Tony Blair (UK), former prime minister; Juan Luis Cebrián (Spain), CEO of *El País*/Prisa;
Rodrigo de Rato (Spain), former managing director of
the IMF; Jacques Delors (France), former president of
the European Commission; Felipe González (Spain),
former prime minister; and Ottmar Issing (Germany), a
former member of the Executive Board of the European
Central Bank; Jakob Kellenberger (Switzerland), former
foreign minister; Alain Minc (France), public intellectual and entrepreneur; Mario Monti (Italy), economist,
former European Commissioner, and (at this writing)
prime minister; Romano Prodi (Italy), former prime minister; Gerhard Schroeder (Germany), former chancellor;
Matti Vanhanen (Finland), former prime minister; and
Guy Verhofstadt (Belgium), former prime minister.

The group also draws on the expertise of other members, including Mohammed El-Erian (CEO of PIMCO);
Niall Ferguson (Harvard University); Anthony Giddens
(former director of the London School of Economics);
Ed Mundell (Nobel laureate in economics and father of
the euro); Nouriel Roubini (financial analyst); Michael

Spence (Nobel laureate, Stanford University); and Joseph Stiglitz (Nobel laureate, Columbia University).

A federal Europe with legitimate governing institutions can be achieved only by the same means that we've advocated elsewhere in this book – through devolving, involving, and decision-division, which has long been known in the European discourse as "subsidiarity," or *only* taking up responsibilities at a higher level that can't be fulfilled at a lower level.

Inescapably, the constitutional mix that will rebalance Europe is different than either California or the G-20 since it already has a meritocratically based governing body, the European Commission, which can attain the authority and legitimacy it needs only by becoming accountable to the elected European Parliament, thus closing the "democratic deficit."

Proponents of a federal Europe will have to make their case to an increasingly reticent public based not only on the benefits of a united Europe with the world's largest market and free mobility of labor and capital, but also on the geopolitical challenges of the world we are heading into instead of the Eurocentric one gone by.

Europe must pull together to compete or be left behind, not only in economic terms, but as a matter of civilizational influence, as power shifts further east to China and a Pacific-oriented America. As former British Prime Minister Tony Blair has put it,* the European project today is less about peace on the Continent, as it was in the 20th century, than about power within the new global system.

Especially in the wake of the euro crisis, former

* Unless otherwise noted, direct quotes in this chapter were taken from a meeting of the Council on the Future of Europe, at the Baur au Lac Hotel in Zurich, January 23, 2012.

Polish Premier Marek Belka has insightfully observed, Europeans have come to see the euro as "amplifying the dislocations of globalization" instead of shielding Europe from them, handing their economic fate over to financial markets and their jobs to "economic enemies" such as China. A competitive Europe that can reap the benefits of globalization instead of suffering the losses that disunity and weakness invite, argues Belka, can be achieved only through political union. "It's pooled sovereignty versus hyper-globalization," he says.

Anyone ambitiously contemplating a federal Europe must be humbled by the historic comparisons. Successful federations of the past have not had the cultural and linguistic obstacles to overcome that face the EU. At its moment of federation in the 1780s, the United States was a sparsely populated handful of young states with a common British culture and one English language. The other great example of successful federation is Switzerland, right in the heart of Europe itself. But even then the Swiss federation was centuries in the making.

"Federation needs time," says Jakob Kellenberger, now chair of the International Red Cross. "It took centuries for people living in Swiss cantons to get to know each other, then a long period of confederation before the move toward full federation in 1848. That transition was made only following an historical moment of great tensions between liberals and conservatives, Protestants and Catholics."

The Swiss federation has worked, says Kellenberger, because the center has been respectful of the autonomy of the cantons, which were never anxious to hand over competencies. The central authorities have been very "prudent" never to abuse their powers. This prudent balance is key to Switzerland's success.

In Switzerland, the division of competencies is very

clear between the federal state and cantons. If a competency is not spelled out in the federal constitution, it belongs to the cantons. Federal competencies include foreign affairs, cultural policy, social policy, and the common domains of economic life such as foreign trade and labor markets.

Any successful long march toward federation must start by fixing the constitutional failings that led to the sovereign debt crisis which now afflicts Europe.

Gerhard Schroeder, the former German chancellor credited with the tough labor market reforms that have made Germany the most competitive country in Europe, traces today's crisis to the faulty decisions made in the heat of the defrosting Cold War order two decades ago. According to Schroeder, then French President François Mitterrand believed that the euro would rein in German power by tying that power to others in the same single currency zone. Then German Chancellor Helmut Kohl, who well understood that a single currency was usually the last, not the first, step in constructing a federal arrangement, nonetheless believed it would one day force political union. Twenty years later, that proposition is being rancorously tested.

Though a young man at the time he was prime minister of Spain, from 1982 to 1996, Felipe González is considered a founding father of the post-Cold War European Union along with Kohl and Mitterrand. He was among the first to warn – now more than a decade ago – that a single currency zone with "divergent, incoherent and uncoordinated" economic policies across nation-states was "preparing the way for asymmetric shocks" such as we've now seen with Greece. One of Europe's smallest states has dragged the whole continent into crisis. Already in 1998, González argued for a common economic union to avert such shocks.

For González, the time has now come for a deliberate, "comprehensive" move to political union that departs from Europe's past pattern of making functional progress through the accumulation of evolutions toward pooled sovereignty – first the Coal and Steel Community, then the Common Agricultural Policy, the customs union, the Common Market, and the incorporation of the central and eastern nations after the fall of the Berlin Wall.

Ottmar Issing, the conservative German economist and a former director of the European Central Bank, agrees. "The single currency should not be seen as a 'back door' to political union," he said recently in Zurich. "If Europe wants a common foreign policy and a political union, it should be directly decided through democratic means."

Jean Pissani-Ferry, the respected head of Bruegel, Europe's top think-tank in Brussels, couldn't agree more. "Kohl's idea was mistaken at its core," he has said. "Money can't create a common identity. Yet, it has nonetheless created interdependence." That interdependence is now threatened, as Pissani-Ferry sees it, because "we have only a weak center of power" in Brussels to manage it. The question now for Europe to move forward is to figure out "what exactly is needed to make a strong, but limited, center?"

This dissonant conundrum of interdependence without a common identity is at the core of the institutional and constitutional challenge to governance everywhere. The double phenomenon of economic convergence yet cultural divergence – the interdependence of plural identities – is the chief characteristic of Globalization 2.0.

Coming from a small, homogeneous country, former Finnish Prime Minister Matti Vanhanen argues that, for Europe, "Identity must precede institutions or they will fail." That proposition is closely related to the other institutional challenge we have discussed in this book: legitimacy is rooted in proximity, since identity has historically been a function of the earthy virtue of place.

When once asked how he would account for the prosperity of the Scandinavian nations despite their high tax rates, Milton Friedman[2] responded that it was because the common identity of an homogeneous culture enables consensus to emerge. In such circumstances, the market is less important. The importance of the market, Friedman said, is precisely that it allows those without a common identity, even those who hate each other, to work together.

Yet, where markets go, institutions must follow because of the interdependence (opportunities, dislocations, externalities) they create among people of different identities. *The challenge today is precisely how to establish effective institutions of governance based on the common interests of interdependence but not preceded by common identity.*

By definition, those institutions must be limited to providing those public goods that are in the common interest without commanding full cultural allegiance or intervention in the autonomous life of nations beyond what is required to sustain the beneficial links of interdependence. It is a matter of scale and competencies. To return to our theme, it is about devolving, involving, and decision-division.

What all this suggests for Europe is that it must first go through a long period of "soft federation" – a strong but limited center with highly autonomous national members – before it arrives at the destination of a federal state that is far lighter than the Leviathan once imagined before the age of distributed power.

All who look toward a federal solution for Europe understand that the starting point must be homogenizing regulation and control of financial institutions operating in the Europe Union. As Felipe González argues, "It is ridiculous for member states to maintain different rules in this common and integrated space where financial institutions operate freely. The absence of homogeneous regulation will only sow the seeds of the next financial crisis and hobble Europe in the decades ahead as it faces new competitive challenges in the global economy."

Also, for González, federalizing economic and fiscal policies is a priority. The various countries should agree to common balance of payments requirements and harmonized minimum taxation. Such a move would make self-evident the need within individual countries to adopt deep structural reforms – for example, more flexibility in rigid labor markets – to help promote competitiveness.

All this is easier said than done because of the diversity of economic models across the EU, from Scandinavia to Italy, including both low-tax, high-consumption economies, such as Greece, and high-tax, low-consumption economies, such as Germany.

For pro-federalists like Guy Verhofstadt, Jacques Delors, and Romano Prodi, aligning European states more closely on such issues as wage levels, the social contract, or tax rates should be the task of the European Commission – which represents all 27 members of the EU – rather than the product of "intergovernmental treaties" inevitably dominated by the larger states, France and Germany – mostly the latter.

"Given the diversity among Europe's economies we do not envisage a one-size-fits-all policy," the trio wrote in the *Financial Times* in 2011.[3] "Rather, we need a clear and united path to convergence on an agreed set of policy measures. Presenting proposals to this end should be the task of the Commission." They went on to say:

> For each proposed measure the Commission should establish – with the agreement of the member states and the European Parliament – a range of standards or goals, within which member states are expected to converge by a given date – for example on the retirement age and a common corporate tax base. The same would be true of R&D investment levels, and wage to productivity ratios.
>
> Progress would have to be regularly monitored, again by the Commission, which should have the power to apply pressure (and ultimately sanctions) for non-compliance, just as it does for breaches of competition rules or infringements of internal market legislation.

If the European Commission – now appointed by the European Council, which consists of the heads of state of all EU members – is to take on the role ascribed to it by Delors and the others, it will need to find a legitimacy it does not now have.

As we have said, the crisis of governance on the Continent today is not so much about the euro as it is about Europe. It is as much about the democratic deficit as it is about the sovereign debt.

National governments have the democratic legitimacy of a popular mandate. Understandably, but narrowly, accountable to their own electorate above all, national leaders have failed to take "ownership" of Europe despite sharing a common currency. The collective result has been to invite financial collapse.

Only more integration and close coordination of policies can restore the health of Europe's balance sheet and sustain stability and prosperity in the long term. But the Europe-wide institutions of integration in Brussels lack a popular mandate, and thus lack the legitimacy to be effective.

Reconciling integration with democracy is the only answer for Europe. And that can be achieved only within the framework of a federal political union in which a democratically elected European Parliament elects, and thus can hold directly accountable, the executive of the European Commission. Such a federation must have a strong center with limited powers checked by strong member states. To that end, the present Council of Europe would be transformed into an "upper house," like the German Bundesrat or the American Senate, as the counterpart to the "lower house" of the current Parliament.

Each policy response to the sovereign debt crisis over the past two years has moved the European Union toward greater integration. The early talk of "robust coordination" has yielded to a fierce debate over how much national sovereignty should be surrendered to a true fiscal union required to sustain the Eurozone. The logical conclusion of this process is a full-fledged political union.

Absent a credible path to that end the crisis will only resurface again and again as each incremental step proves insufficient. In short, the resolution of the sovereign debt crisis and the ultimate convergence of economic conditions, as both Angela Merkel and Mario Monti have publicly acknowledged, can only be accomplished by returning to the task of "deepening" Europe through the establishment of a full-fledged federal union.

The time has surely arrived to also look beyond the immediate horizon and start thinking through what the new governing institutions of such a political union might look like.

This is a challenge not only for Europe's leaders but, above all, for an engaged public. Only their full involvement can lend the requisite legitimacy to the institutions

of the European Union, whose effectiveness is hobbled
by the present "democratic deficit."

As we have already made clear, any effort to design
the pooling of sovereignty in a political union must
focus on limiting the power of a federal European
government to provision of the necessary European
public goods – such as macroeconomic coordination,
common infrastructure, and foreign affairs – while leaving most functions from education or cultural policies
with the sovereign states. While member states must
retain flexibility in the policy mix they choose, they
would be required to maintain balanced budgets, as
with the American states or the fiscal pact agreed by the
Eurozone states in December 2011.

Europe's identity will always come from diversity,
not uniformity or excessive centralization. No one
wants homogeneity. It especially makes little sense to
overbuild a bureaucratic edifice in Brussels in an information age where the distributed power of networks is
transforming the nature of governance itself.

Though a federal Europe would be open to all, the
imperative of moving toward political union should
not be held back by those not willing to move forward.
The democratic publics of each state will have to decide
whether it is in their long-term interest to join the federation, or opt out. It is an illusion to believe that a strong
political union can be built on the weak allegiance that
results from tweaking treaties. Its foundation must be a
popular mandate.

In the spirit of starting this critical debate, here is an
outline sketch of what political union in Europe might
look like (see also Figure 8.1):

1 The European Parliament would elect the chief
   executive of the European Commission, who would

Europe

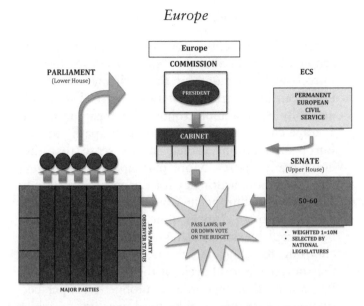

Figure 8.1 An outline sketch of what political union in Europe might look like (courtesy of Alexander Gardels)

form a cabinet of ministers out of the larger parties in the Parliament, including a finance minister with the capacity to levy taxes and formulate a budget on a Europe-wide basis with substantially more resources than the current 1 percent of EU GDP. The finance minister's focus would be on macroeconomic coordination, not microeconomic management. Other cabinet post competencies would be limited to provision of supranational "European public goods" (defense, foreign policy, energy, infrastructure, etc.), leaving as many decisions on other matters as possible in the hands of national governments within the federation.

2 The European Court of Justice would arbitrate when sovereign issues of the federal government and the nation-state are in dispute.

3 Because of the enhanced power of the Parliament to

select a chief executive for Europe who will be the center of accountability – "the euro stops here" – Europe-wide elections for the Parliament based on European lists instead of national party lists would naturally become more robust and engaging for the average citizen, replacing the present apathy toward European elections rooted in the sense that they don't really matter. More participation by citizens will mean more legitimacy for European institutions.

4 The current European Council would be transformed into an "upper house." Members would be selected by nation-states in the manner of their choosing for staggered terms that are longer than the shorter electoral cycle of the lower house of the Parliament, thus encouraging a longer-term perspective on governance. Unlike the lower house, which is primarily focused on the short-term interests of its national constituents, the upper house should be a deliberative body focused on the long-term, big picture of Europe in the world. All member states would have representation, either through a proportional system based on population or, like the US Senate, two representatives per state.

5 In order to preserve some of the nonpartisan meritocratic quality of the current Commission, each cabinet minister in the Commission would be paired with a permanent secretary from the European Civil Service in their area of competence.

6 As in an ideal "Westminster system," the formulation of budgets would rest with the Commission, not with the Parliament. The Commission budget would be presented for an up or down vote in the Parliament and not subject to special-interest "horse trading" through the legislative process. A vote of no-confidence by the Parliament may reject the

policy direction set by the Commission, in which case a new government would be formed.

7 Taxes and legislation would have to be approved by a majority of both the Parliament and the upper house.

8 In order to promote a "consensus majority" in the Parliament, parties that obtained less than 10 percent of the vote in Europe-wide elections would be present in debate, but not vote. Such a rule would tend to push politics toward centrist compromise and avoid gridlock that might arise from the veto power of small parties in a coalition.

To be sure, there are many questions outstanding about moving toward a political union. To foster legitimacy, mustn't these institutions and their rules be established from the bottom up through a Constituent Assembly rather than by a treaty change? Would the large parties that win the most seats in the European Parliament have sufficiently common agendas to be able to form consensus and govern? At an even more fundamental level, as we discussed earlier, can a political union ever truly cohere if not preceded by European nation-building aimed at forging a common identity based as much on a shared sense of purpose for the future as on the diverse heritage of the past?

Federal arrangements in other polities such as Switzerland and the US have proven to be highly beneficial and enduring.

In 1789, then US Secretary of the Treasury Alexander Hamilton proposed a strong federal system of government that would assume the states' debts from the American Revolution while guaranteeing a steady future revenue stream, further integrating fiscal policy while preserving a large swath of local sovereignty on non-federal issues. This was the first step in making the United States a continental and ultimately a global power.

So too in Europe in 2012, debt resolution will be the midwife of a political union that could make Europe a powerful pillar in the multi-polar geopolitical order of the 21st century. The only way to answer this challenge in the face of the uncertainties we mention is for Europe's leaders, and its public, to at last commit to this transformation instead of remaining paralyzed with hesitancy.

Part III

Conclusion

9

Survival of the Wisest

Despite the daunting obstacles we've reported, our experiences in California, Europe, and at the G-20 level suggest that structural change along the lines of intelligent governance is as possible as it is necessary.

As we have argued throughout this book, the common challenges humanity has created for itself as we forge the first truly global civilization can be resolved only by drawing on the collective practical wisdom of both West and East while employing the game-changing technologies of the information age. For the first time in history, governing hierarchies are being horizontally widened to the point where the broad middle have the same access to power as their rulers. Unlike land or propertied assets, the possession of knowledge is not zero-sum: it can be shared by all and lift all horizons.

Humankind has come a long way in the past 5,000 years. Never have so many lived so well and so freely for so long, traveled so far and experienced so much. We know how to transplant organs, clone creatures, regenerate cells, and instantly flash data around the world through fiber-optic cables or satellite signals. We can even peer into the distant origins of the universe.

Yet, our systems of governance so far have lagged

behind in organizing a good society that works for all. Vast inequality and illiteracy persist. Half of humanity still lives in poverty. Billions lack basic freedoms, not to mention the requisite minimums for personal self-realization. All too often, violence remains the favored manner to settle scores and disputes.

Paradoxically, our own creations threaten what we've accomplished. Nuclear weapons are still plentiful and proliferating. With a population of seven billion and counting, the very prosperity achieved though widespread industrialization is depleting finite resources and threatening to upset the ecological balance that has enabled humanity to flourish within the narrow band of earth's livable climate.

As humankind enters what scientists now call the anthropocene age – the first era of the earth's long history in which our species is the dominant influence – we are obliged to establish a new equilibrium that brings the way in which we govern ourselves up to par with our scientific and technological leaps and their manifold consequences.

In many ways, the faster, wealthier, more connected, and more complex our scientific and technological civilization, the less intelligent our governance of it has become.

What Henri Bergson[1] said of the spirit is also true of the "spirit of laws," as Montesquieu[2] called his treatise on governance. In the "disproportionately magnified body" of technological society, Bergson observed, "the soul remains what it was, too small to fill it, and too feeble to direct it."[3] Growing to fit that role with smart governance is the foremost challenge.

No silver bullet of salvation is going to fix all our problems. All we have to go on is what has been tried and tested by history – both the remarkable millennia-long resilience of China's "institutional civilization" and the brief and shining moment of liberal democracy.

Intelligent governance is the new civic software that can make these different operating systems more compatible. Its chief aim is to seek a harmonious equilibrium in human affairs – between responsibility and personal choice, community and the individual, freedom and stability, well-being and well-having, humankind and nature, present and future – based on the wisdom of what has worked best when faced with the circumstances at hand.

It is a given that any universal approach that arises from new global conditions must pragmatically accommodate diversity and varying levels of development. Cooperation, which implies different paths to the same end, not the lock-step uniformity of one model, is the means to achieve harmonious collaboration. From the shattering of the Tower of Babel to the collapse of the Soviet Union, history has taught us that diversity is the way of human nature.

Such mutually beneficial cooperation is more possible today than at any previous point in human history. Some scientists argue that the capacity to share knowledge across cultures enabled by the "global thinking circuit" of our wired world and the planetary reach of the media is akin to "horizontal gene transfer." This suggests that rule by more intelligence sharing instead of competitive differentiation might mark an "evolution of evolution."

When joined with the knowledge explosion in science and the information revolution, the necessity for all of humanity to work together for survival raises the hope that our species will graduate from the primitive, competitive mode of human evolution – "survival of the fittest" – to a less conflictive, more intelligent, and more

183

Conclusion

cooperative mode – "survival of the wisest." Intelligent governance is, in this sense, the practical application of an evolved worldview.

Bowing to the historical seniority of the East, that worldview might be called harmonism. It is perhaps the 21st-century alternative to a narrow notion of "progress" that, while achieving fantastic leaps forward, has also brought much damage in the wake of its ambitions – extinguished cultural diversity, sacrificed lives, and a degraded environment. While harmonism doesn't regret the future, neither does it imagine a utopia at some end-point in history. Rather, it constantly strives for a state of equilibrium.

Whether the various crises that have arisen today can be met with the awareness and spirit of cooperation we propose will certainly test the maturity of civilization. Our tempered hope is that a world in which the "East and West" inhabit each other, and in which individuals everywhere share the same access to the means of power as their rulers, will meet that test.

Notes

Chapter 1 Globalization 2.0 and the Challenges to Good Governance

1 G.W.F. Hegel, *Philosophy of History*, trans. J. Sibree, New York: American Home Library Company, 1902 [1837].
2 F. Fukuyama, *The End of History and the Last Man*, New York: Simon and Schuster, 2006 [1992].
3 M. Wolf, "In the Grip of a Great Convergence," *Financial Times*, January 4, 2011.
4 M. Spence, *The Next Convergence: The Future of Economic Growth in a Multispeed World*, New York: Farrar, Straus and Giroux, 2011, pp. 4–5.
5 J.A. Schumpeter, *Capitalism, Socialism and Democracy*, 3rd edn, New York: Harper Perennial, 1962.
6 D. Stockman, "Moyers & Company: David Stockman on Crony Capitalism," interview by Bill Moyers, January 20, 2012. Accessed at: http://billmoyers.com/segment/david-stockman-on-crony-capitalism/ (May 2012).
7 C. Freeland, "US Workers Pay as Jobs Go Global," *International Herald-Tribune*, February 3, 2012.
8 C. Duhigg and K. Bradsher, "How the US Lost Out on iPhone Work," *New York Times*, February 3, 2012.
9 Spence, *The Next Convergence*.
10 R. Rajan, *Fault Lines: How Hidden Fractures Still*

Threaten the World Economy, Princeton: Princeton University Press, 2010.

Chapter 2 America's Consumer Democracy versus China's Modern Mandarinate

1 Zhang Weiwei, *The China Wave: The Rise of a Civilizational State*, Hackensack, NJ: World Century, 2012.

2 Pan Wei, "Origins of the Min-bei System," presented at The Idea of Political Meritocracy: A Nanyang Technological University Interdisciplinary Symposium, Nanyang Technological University, Singapore, January 6–8, 2012.

3 N. Gardels, "Deglobalization or Market Pluralism?" *New Perspectives Quarterly*, 16(1) (1999), pp. 2–3.

4 F. Fukuyama, *The End of History and the Last Man*, New York: Simon and Schuster, 2006.

5 F. Fukuyama, "US Democracy Has Little to Teach China," *Financial Times*, January 17, 2011.

6 M. Wolf, "Lunch with the FT: Francis Fukuyama," *Financial Times*, May 27, 2011.

7 F. Fukuyama, discussion at the Nicolas Berggruen Institute, Rosewood Sandhill Resort, Menlo Park, CA, December 4, 2011.

8 M. Olson, *The Rise and Decline of Nations: Economic Growth, Stagflation, and Social Rigidities*, New Haven, CT: Yale University Press, 1984.

9 E.X. Li, "Why China's Political Model Is Superior," *New York Times*, February 16, 2012.

10 Kenich Ohmae, interview by Nathan Gardels, January 9, 2012.

11 "Banyan: The Party Goes On," *The Economist*, May 28, 2009.

12 Y. Yevtushenko, "Russia's Pink Clouds of Utopia," in N. Gardels (ed.), *The Changing World Order: World*

Leaders Reflect, Malden, MA: Blackwell Publishers, Inc., 1997, pp. 119–22.

13 D. Stockman, "David Stockman on Crony Capitalism," BillMoyers.com, March 9, 2012. Accessed at: http://billmoyers.com/segment/david-stockman-on-crony-capitalism/ (May 2012).

14 G. Soros, *The New Paradigm for Financial Markets: The Credit Crisis of 2008 and What It Means*, New York: PublicAffairs, 2008.

15 D. Bell, *The Cultural Contradictions of Capitalism*, 20th anniversary edn, New York: Basic Books, 1996.

16 D. Moyo, *How the West Was Lost: Fifty Years of Economic Folly – and the Smart Choices Ahead*, New York: Farrar, Straus and Giroux, 2011.

17 M.A. Hiltzik, *Colossus: Hoover Dam and the Making of the American Century*, New York: Free Press, 2010.

18 Quoted in N. Berggruen, "From California to Greece, Governance is the Key Issue," Forbes.com, May 28, 2010. Accessed at: http://www.forbes.com/2010/05/28/nicolas-berggruen-billionaire-california-china-government.html (May 2012).

19 R. Frazier, "CA Spends More on Prisons Than Schools," PressTV.com, June 21, 2011. Accessed at: http://www.presstv.ir/detail/185641.html (May 2012).

20 Berggruen, "From California to Greece."

21 Nicolas Berggruen Institute, *A Blueprint to Renew California: Report and Recommendations Presented by the Think Long Committee for California*, Beverly Hills, CA, 2011.

22 A. Kluth, "Democracy in California: The People's Will," *The Economist*, April 23, 2011.

23 S. Roach, "The Next China," *Aspenia*, 15 (2010), pp. 38–43.

24 S. Huntington, *Political Order in Changing Societies*, New Haven, CT: Yale University Press, 2006.

25 J. Woetzel, J. Devan, L. Jordan, S. Negri, and D. Farrell,

"Preparing for China's Urban Billion," McKinsey Global Institute, March 2008.

26 G. Yeo, "China's Megacity Mandarinate," *New Perspectives Quarterly*, 27(3) (2010), pp. 40–3.
27 "Fareed Zakaria GPS: Interview with Wen Jiabao," CNN.com, October 3, 2010. Accessed at: http://tran scripts.cnn.com/TRANSCRIPTS/1010/03/fzgps.01.html (May 2012).
28 Conversation with He Baogang and Nathan Gardels, January 7, 2012.
29 F. Fukuyama and Zhang Weiwei, "The China Model: A Dialogue between Francis Fukuyama and Zhang Weiwei," *New Perspectives Quarterly*, 28(4) (2011), pp. 40–67.
30 Ibid., pp. 41–2.
31 Ibid., p. 45.
32 Ibid., p. 45.
33 Ibid., p. 46.
34 Ibid., p. 48.
35 Ibid., p. 51.
36 Ibid., pp. 58–9.
37 Ibid., p. 64.
38 Huntington, *Political Order in Changing Societies*.

Chapter 3 Liberal Democratic Constitutionalism and Meritocracy: Hybrid Possibilities

1 J. Rawls, *A Theory of Justice*, revised edition, Cambridge, MA: Harvard University Press, 1999.
2 H.G. Creel, *Confucius: The Man and the Myth*, Whitefish, MT: Kessinger Publishing, 2010, pp. 275–6.
3 Ibid., p. 276.
4 Ibid., p. 256.
5 Ibid., pp. 260–1.
6 Ibid., p. 268.
7 Ibid., p. 269.
8 Ibid., p. 256.
9 Y. Pines, "Between Merit and Pedigree: Evolution of the

Concept of 'Elevating the Worth' in Pre-imperial China," presented at The Idea of Political Meritocracy: A Nanyang Technological University Interdisciplinary Symposium, Nanyang Technological University, Singapore, January 6–8, 2012.

10 Ibid.

11 "Italy Crisis: Mario Monti Appointed New PM-Designate," BBC News, November 13, 2011. Accessed at: http://www.bbc.co.uk/news/world-europe-15713985 (May 2012).

12 J. Hooper, "Mario Monti Appoints Technocrats to Steer Italy Out of Economic Crisis," *Guardian*, November 16, 2011.

13 M. Olson, *The Rise and Decline of Nations: Economic Growth, Stagflation, and Social Rigidities*, New Haven, CT: Yale University Press, 1984.

14 Pan Wei, interview by Nathan Gardels, Beijing, January 10, 2012.

15 J. Madison, "The Federalist No. 10: The Utility of the Union as a Safeguard Against Domestic Faction and Insurrection," *Daily Advertiser*, November 22, 1787.

16 S. Macedo, "Political Meritocracy and Liberal Democratic Constitutionalism," presented at The Idea of Political Meritocracy: A Nanyang Technological University Interdisciplinary Symposium, Nanyang Technological University, Singapore, January 6–8, 2012.

17 J. Madison, "The Federalist No. 62: The Senate," *Independent Journal*, February 27, 1788.

18 A. Hamilton, "The Federalist No. 68: The Mode of Electing the President," *Independent Journal*, March 12, 1788.

19 Macedo, "Political Meritocracy and Liberal Democratic Constitutionalism."

20 M. Lind, "A Sino-Hellenic Humanism," *New Perspectives Quarterly*, 17(4) (2000), pp. 58–61 (p. 58).

21 Ibid., p. 60.

22 H. Kissinger, *On China*, New York: Penguin Press, 2011, p. 13.

23 Lind, "A Sino-Hellenic Humanism," p. 59.
24 Ibid., p. 59.
25 M. Wolf, "In the Grip of a Great Convergence," *Financial Times*, January 4, 2011.
26 E.X. Li, "Globalization 2.0: Democracy's Coming Demise," Huffington Post, February 19, 2012. Accessed at: http://www.huffingtonpost.com/eric-x-li/globalization-20-democrac_b_1278784.html (May 2012).
27 See Zhang's *The China Wave: Rise of a Civilizational State*, Hackensack, NJ: World Century, 2012.
28 D.A. Bell, "Moving Eastward," *New York Times*, February 16, 2011.
29 Bai Tongdong, "A Confucian Version of Hybrid Regime: How Does It Work and Why Is It Superior?" presented at The Idea of Political Meritocracy: A Nanyang Technological University Interdisciplinary Symposium, Nanyang Technological University, Singapore, January 6–8, 2012.
30 J. Rawls, *Political Liberalism*, New York: Columbia University Press, 2005.
31 J. Brennan, *The Ethics of Voting*, New York: Princeton University Press, 2012, p. 176.
32 Quoted in B. Obama, *The Audacity of Hope: Thoughts on Reclaiming the American Dream*, New York: Random House Digital, Inc., 2006, p. 135.
33 M.E. Warren and H. Pearse, *Designing Deliberative Democracy: The British Columbia Citizens' Assembly*, New York: Cambridge University Press, 2008.
34 Bai Tongdong, "A Confucian Version of Hybrid Regime."

Chapter 4 The New Challenges for Governance: Social Networks, Megacities, and the Global Scattering of Productive Capabilities

1 "Zuckerberg Explains Facebook's Mission in Letter to Investors," *New York Daily News*, February 1, 2012.
2 D. Brin, *The Transparent Society: Will Technology*

Force Us to Choose Between Privacy and Freedom?, Cambridge, MA: Basic Books, 1999.

3 K. Marx, *Das Kapital: A Critique of Political Economy*, ed. F. Engels and S.L. Levitsky, Washington, DC: Regnery Gateway, 1996 [1867].

4 K. Nahon, "Fuzziness of Inclusion/Exclusion in Networks," *International Journal of Communications*, 4 (2011), pp. 756–72.

5 See note 2.

6 E.X. Li and G. Yeo, "China's Parallel Universe," *South China Morning Post*, January 20, 2012.

7 J. Keane, "China's Labyrinth," *South China Morning Post*, February 20, 2012.

8 A. Gramsci, *Prison Notebooks*, ed. and trans. A. Buttigieg, New York: Columbia University Press, 2010 [1929–35].

9 R. Jacob and Z. Ping, "Wukan's Young Activists Embrace New Role," *Financial Times*, February 12, 2012.

10 S. LaFraniere, "A Grass-Roots Fight to Save a 'Super-Tree,'" *New York Times*, June 4, 2011.

11 M. Sanchanta and M. Obe, "Moms Turn Activists in Japanese Crisis," WSJ.com, June 17, 2011. Accessed at: http://online.wsj.com/article/SB10001424052702303499 204576389094076351276.html (May 2012).

12 J. Dempsey, "Enraged Citizens' Movement Rattles German Politics," *New York Times*, May 6, 2011.

13 R. Donadio, "Italian Voters Come Out to Overturn Laws and Deliver a Rebuke to Berlusconi," *New York Times*, June 13, 2011.

14 G. Tremlett and J. Hooper, "Protest in the Med: Rallies against Cuts and Corruption Spread," *Guardian*, May 19, 2011.

15 N. Gardels, *New York Summary Report: 21st Century Council Meeting, New York March 26–27*, New York: Nicolas Berggruen Institute, 2011.

16 "David Cameron: We Are Creating a New Era of Transparency," *The Telegraph*, 6 July 2011.

17 N. Gardels, transcript of the Berlin Meeting of the

NBI 21st Century Council, Berlin: Nicolas Berggruen Institute, 2010.

18 D. Brin, "On 'Gin, Television, and Cognitive Surplus: A Talk by Clay Shirky'," Edge.com, 2008. Accessed at: http://www.edge.org/discourse/cognitive_surplus. html#brind (May 2012).

19 N. Gardels, "Media and Politics: From Machiavelli to Zeffirelli in Italy," *Washington Post*, May 14, 1999.

20 G. de Michelis, "Beyond Newtonian Democracy," *New Perspectives Quarterly*, 9(4) (1992), pp. 9–11.

21 David Brin, interview by Nathan Gardels, February 13, 2012.

22 Ibid.

23 Tung Cheehwa, interview by Nathan Gardels and Nicolas Berggruen, November 2011.

24 M. Castells, *The Informational City: Information Technology, Economic Restructuring, and the Urban-regional Process*, Malden, MA: Wiley-Blackwell, 1991.

25 M. Castells, *The Rise of the Network Society: The Information Age: Economy, Society, and Culture*, Blackwell Publishers, Malden, MA, 2011 [1996].

26 M. Castells, "Megacities and the End of Urban Civilization," *New Perspectives Quarterly*, 13(3) (1996), pp. 12–14 (p. 12).

27 F. Holmes, "Middle-Class Middleweights to Be Growth Champions," Frank Holmes' Instablog, March 30, 2011. Accessed at: http://seekingalpha.com/instablog/389729-frank-holmes/158671-middle-class-middleweights-to-be-growth-champions-bookmark-and-share (May 2012).

28 R. Koolhaas, *Content*, Berlin: Taschen, 2004.

29 Quoted in N. Gardels, "The Generic City: Singapore or Bladerunner?" *New Perspectives Quarterly*, 13(3) (1996), pp. 4–9 (p. 9).

30 Quoted in ibid., p. 7.

31 G. Yeo, "China's Megacity Mandarinate," *New Perspectives Quarterly*, 17(4) (2010), pp. 40–3.

32 P. Soleri, "The Frugal City," *New Perspectives Quarterly*, 17(4) (2000), pp. 4–8.
33 Gardels, *New York Summary Report*.
34 D. Bell and A. De-Shalit, "From Nationalism to Civicism," *New Perspectives Quarterly*, 29(1) (2012), pp. 57–60 (p. 58).
35 Quoted in N. Gardels, "Singapore: Post-Liberal City of the Future," in N. Gardels (ed.),*The Changing Global Order: World Leaders Reflect*, Malden, MA: Blackwell Publishers, Inc., 1997, pp. 244–50 (p. 244).
36 J. Gray, "*Modus Vivendi*: Liberalism for the Coming Middle Ages," *New Perspectives Quarterly*, 18(2) (2001), pp. 4–21 (p. 19).
37 J. Woetzel, J. Devan, L. Jordan, S. Negri, and D. Farrell, "Preparing for China's Urban Billion," McKinsey Global Institute, March 2008.
38 P. Lamy, "Change the Way the World Measures Trade," *New Perspectives Quarterly*, 29(2) (2012), pp. 37–8.
39 Ibid., pp. 38–9.
40 N. Gardels, *Pre-G20 Summit Forum: 21st Century Council Summary Report*, Paris: Nicolas Berggruen Institute, October 2011.
41 Lamy, "Change the Way the World Measures Trade," p. 3.
42 Gardels, *Pre-G20 Summit Forum*.
43 Alvin Toffler, *The Third Wave*, New York: Random House, 1987.

Chapter 5 Intelligent Governance: Tenets and Template

1 K. Marx, *Das Kapital: A Critique of Political Economy*, ed. F. Engels and S.L. Levitsky, Washington, DC: Regnery Gateway, 1996 [1867].
2 J. Rawls, *A Theory of Justice*, revised edn, Cambridge, MA: Harvard University Press, 1999.
3 From an interview with the authors, San Francisco, March 4, 2011.

4 F. Bastiat, *Selected Essays on Political Economy*, New York: Van Nostrand, 1964, cited in B.D. Caplan, *The Myth of the Rational Voter: Why Democracies Choose Bad Policies*, Princeton: Princeton University Press, 2008, p. 197.
5 Pan Wei, interview by Nathan Gardels, January 10, 2012.
6 R. Brookhiser, *James Madison*, New York: Basic Books, 2012, p. 98.
7 See, for example, A.M. Schlesinger Jr., *The Cycles of American History*, New York: Houghton Mifflin Harcourt, 1999.
8 He Baogang, interview by Nathan Gardels, January 7, 2012.

Chapter 6 Rebooting California's Dysfunctional Democracy

1 N. Berggruen, *A Blueprint to Renew California: Report and Recommendations Presented by the Think Long Committee for California*, Los Angeles: Nicolas Berggruen Institute, 2011.
2 California Forward, The Government Performance and Accountability Act, 2012. Accessed at: http://www.cafwd-action.org/pages/proposed-ballot-measure (May 2012).
3 C.W. Simmons, *California's Statewide Initiative Process*, Sacramento: California Research Bureau, California State Library, 1997.
4 A. Kluth, "Democracy in California: The People's Will," *The Economist*, April 23, 2011.
5 Ibid.
6 F. Fukuyama, *The Origins of Political Order: From Prehuman Times to the French Revolution*, New York: Macmillan, 2011, p. 452.
7 M. Olson, *The Rise and Decline of Nations: Economic Growth, Stagflation, and Social Rigidities*, New Haven, CT: Yale University Press, 1984.

8 D.G. Savage and P. McGreevy, "US Supreme Court Orders Massive Inmate Release to Relieve California's Crowded Prisons," *Los Angeles Times*, May 24, 2011.

Chapter 7 The G-20: Global Governance from Summits to Subnational Networks

1 N. Gardels, *Pre-G20 Summit Forum: 21st Century Council Summary Report*, Paris: Nicolas Berggruen Institute, 2011.
2 Zheng Bijian, "China's 'Peaceful Rise' to Great-Power Status," *Foreign Affairs*, September 1, 2005.
3 Zheng Bijian, "Building Communities of Interest," in *Briefing Book: Globalization 2.0 and the Future of the G-20*, New York: 21st Century Council, Nicolas Berggruen Institute, February 18, 2011, pp. 32–3.
4 Shi Yu, "China's 12th Five Year Plan: A Preliminary Look, Part II," *Beijing Today*, March 8, 2011.
5 Quoted in N. Gardels, "21st Century Council Concept Paper," in *Briefing Book: Globalization 2.0 and the Future of the G20*.
6 Ibid., pp. 8–9.
7 Ibid., p. 9.
8 Ibid., p. 10.
9 D. Siders, "Capitol Alert: Jerry Brown Plans Trip to China to Court Investors," *The Sacramento Bee*, February 25, 2012.
10 D. Siders, "Jerry Brown Seeks Chinese Investments for California Projects," *The Sacramento Bee*, March 2, 2012.

Chapter 8 Europe: Political Union and the Democratic Deficit

1 H.M. Enzensberger, *Brussels, the Gentle Monster: Or the Disenfranchisement of Europe,* trans. Martin Chalmers, Chicago: Seagull Books, 2011.

2 M. Friedman, "Free Markets and the End of History," *New Perspectives Quarterly*, 23(1) (2006), pp. 37–43.
3 G. Verhofstadt, J. Delors, and R. Prodi, "Europe Must Plan a Reform, Not a Pact," *Financial Times*, March 2, 2011.

Chapter 9 Survival of the Wisest

1 H. Bergson, *The Two Sources of Morality and Religion*, trans. R. Audra and C. Bereton, London: Macmillan and Co., 1935 [1932].
2 C. Montesquieu, *The Spirit of Laws*, printed for G. and A. Ewing and G. Faulkner, Dublin, 1751 [1748].
3 Bergson, *The Two Sources of Morality*, p. 268.